Confident Thinking.

Tales, Tips & Techniques
to empower your life.

Su Ainsworth.

Editing services provided by Jackie Dickinson.
Formatting supplied by Graham Clarke.
Cover design by Grace Daryl Mills.
Additional designs provided by A&P.
ISBN 978-0-9928569-3-9.

To contact the author please email suainsworth@gmail.com

Get Your Thinking Right and You Won't Go Far Wrong

When I was a teenager, someone said to me, 'Get your thinking right Susan and you won't go far wrong.' At the time, I didn't understand what they meant but it was a catchy saying and I never forgot it. Incredibly, it wasn't until I entered my forties that I realised I had been given an insightful piece of advice: a real pearl of wisdom, which came into play in my life at just the right moment. Welcome to Confident Thinking.

We all have different thinking styles (which is another book altogether) and in this book, you will learn how to think confidently about everything that comes your way. It is much more than a book about positive thinking because I will also show you how to build an **empowerment toolbox, which** you can open up and use whenever you need it.

I've discovered that **people don't think enough** and, as a result, they slip into stale routines, rarely trying new things. We are all guilty of staying in our comfort zone. On my daily school run, I had to pass a busy school drop-off point, which caused a huge traffic jam each morning. What folk failed to see was that if they allowed cars **out** of the school gate, it would allow more traffic to **move up to enter** the school gate at the other side. But unfortunately, selfishness and blinkered thinking meant that people blanked the parents waiting to leave, causing frustration all around. They couldn't they see the simple solution to free up the traffic **because they weren't thinking.**

If you really want results, you will need to do a lot of thinking as you read through this manual for confidence building!

Forward by Fiona Castle & Rob Whittaker.

This book is filled with encouragement, challenge and bubbling with enthusiasm for making the most of life. I am sure that every reader whether young or old will benefit from Susan's positive motivation and can do attitude. She is honest about her own experiences and difficulties and her own determination to overcome them. She also recognizes the value of her faith as a Christian, to enable her to discover her strengths and gifts. I wish I could have read this book as a teenager! It certainly would have changed my outlook on life and increased my self-worth and confidence. It should be made available in every school library.
Fiona Castle. OBE. Speaker & Writer

What a privilege to be able to unreservedly commend this book to you.
I have known its author, Su, for over a quarter of a century. I've tracked her own growth in the areas she so compellingly describes in these pages. And, I've seen the long term impact in her own life as she has not only said ... but also done the things you are about to read.
What excites me most about this book is its honesty, its vulnerability and its practicality. A well-known preacher once said "I know does not mean I know, until 'I know' gets linked up with I do." There is lots of street wisdom here, but also lots of things to put into practice.
So, buy it, read it and enjoy it. As you begin to build its wisdom into your life, you will slowly but surely turn into the best version of you!
Rob Whittaker. Principal. Capernwray Bible School.

Introduction (don't skip this bit!)

Congratulations

You've invested time in reading this book because you like to keep on learning. I believe that skilled living comes when we devote some time to **think** about how we can improve and be the best possible version of ourselves. The Bible puts it like this:

Wise men and women are always learning, always listening for fresh insights.

(Proverbs 18:15 The Message)

As you read through this set of 4 sessions from my successful *Confidence Gym Course – a Workout for your Self-Esteem*, I will be revealing a lot of information about myself in the form of little stories so I'll do no introduction here, but gradually let it unfold. What I will tell you though is that I'm passionate about helping people get on in life and overcome the obstacles that keep them stuck in mediocrity.

I've worked the title of this book into small icons to show whether it's a tale, tip or technique I'm revealing as you read. I've another T at the back, which are Testimonials from just a few people who have been to Confidence Gym over the years. At the end of each session you'll find a list of Thinking Tools to put in your Empowerment Toolbox.

I started to research my Confidence Gym course in 2002. I didn't know I was going be launching a course at the time, but I felt totally driven to read books about science and the differences between men and women. The amazing thing I want to tell you from the outset is that *all* the confidence-building principles can be found in the Bible. For those of you who are interested, I've included some verses to help you see where these are.

Many of the books I've studied are listed at the back of this book. I borrowed most of them from the library as they can obtain any book that has been printed in the UK and it will cost you very little. Then, if you think it's good, you can decide to buy it. Being a frugal chick, I browse high street bookshops and if I see something interesting, I order it from the library. I won't even mind if you've borrowed my book from the library!

Before you begin, why not click on my website. It will give you a flavour of how I look and speak, my sense of humour, personality and character. I've always found it more interesting when I know the person whose book I'm reading - I can almost hear them speaking the words. It's not compulsory but you will enjoy it more. www.suainsworth.co.uk

YOUR TOOLBOX FOR
Building Confidence

Symbols and Meanings

The butterfly makes the greatest change when it locks its self away to transform. This signifies that some thinking time is required here.

The book signifies a story I'm recounting that makes this real for me hence, the tales part of my title.

This will indicate a method being used. I can't easily move a settee through a maze of rooms, but it is possible with the right technique.

Here's an idea that might work for you.

For everything that was written in the past was written to teach us, so that through the endurance taught in the Scriptures and the encouragement they provide we may have hope.

Romans 15v4 NIV.

You must also read this next bit to get the best out of my book.

The feedback I receive from the course is that the tools and techniques, when used correctly, *will* bring the desired results. In other words, it works!

This leads me to write the most important lines in the book.

Be a 5%er

When I was working in advertising, we attended many training courses. On one such course, the speaker grabbed my attention immediately when he said that 95% of the people in the room were losers!

What - how very dare he! He went on to explain that only 5% of us would actually go on to use the sales techniques he was teaching. His assertion was based on research findings that 95% of people *never action* anything they read or hear. The winners are the 5% who do. The Bible puts it like this:

> **Don't fool yourself into thinking that you are a listener when you are anything but, letting the Word go in one ear and out the other. *Act* on what you hear!**
>
> (James 1:22 The Message)

Something in me clicked. I wasn't going to waste *my* time. I was determined to be a 5%er and that is what I want *you* to be too. Don't make reading this book just another that you will forget all about in time.

USE the information and your life WILL change.

I know that's rather a bold statement but I've had *so much* positive feedback from women determined to be a 5%er. The % symbol sits above the number 5 on your computer keyboard so you have no excuse for forgetting! So let's get started.

Building Confidence

What is confidence.   Page 12

Barriers to building confidence.   Page 28

Building self-esteem.   Page 44

Social confidence.   Page 56

What's my Purpose?

Confidence to go for it.   Page 67

Barriers to fulfilling your destiny.   Page 87

The art of goal setting.   Page 98

Stress Busting

Stress kills Confidence.   Page 112

Memory Helpers.   Page 118

Toxic Emotions.   Page 138

How to Increase Happiness

This is what everyone really wants to know   Page 158

Happiness Additives.   Page 178

How it worked out for me.   Page 189

Thank you to important people   Page 196

Testimonials & how to book a session.   Page 198

Building Confidence

What is confidence?

Basically, it's a belief system. Various other words are used to describe confidence such as *faith, trust,* and *assurance.*

What you believe about yourself is called *self-esteem.*

Confidence comes in many categories, the main ones being:

1. SOCIAL   I'm no good at meeting people.

2. PERSONAL   Nobody likes me (everybody hates me, think I'll go 'n' eat worms!).

3. WORK   What am I good at?

Q If level 10 confidence is running round your garden naked at night and level 1 is you don't like getting out of bed in the morning because you're scared of what you'll face, then where are you on that scale?

We regularly have a 10 on the course and a few 8s and 9s but most are 5, 6 or 7.

Q Taking each of the 3 categories, capture a *moment to think* about the areas you would like to improve.

Research shows that when it comes to confidence, *no one has it all together*. It's normal to feel a little inadequate at certain times in our lives. Right now, you may think you can conquer the world but, in a year's time, you may fall apart at the seams just as I did when I was 24. My husband of 3 years came home after starting a new job and told me he'd never really loved me and wanted a divorce. I'll tell you more about what happened later but, as you can imagine, my *personal* confidence took a nosedive. I was being dumped and it hurt like hell so to compensate, I threw myself into something I knew I was good at - my work. How I used to feel about *myself* disappeared overnight and, slowly but surely, I began to withdraw. That's why it is helpful if you can identify which of the 3 areas you'd like to start work on.

Warning

This first session is rather like chewing a tough steak (apologies to the vegetarians). A bit of learning is required in order to understand HOW our minds work. When you understand that, you will know HOW the formula I'll give you is going to work.

When I was little and my parents gave me steak, I used to push it all down the plughole in the kitchen sink because I couldn't be bothered chewing it. My aunt Margaret also used to find it stuffed under cushions in her dining room. Let's be honest, none of us like hard work but some things are good for us. Steak for building our bodies and knowledge for building our minds. Get ready to chew!

To build confidence, we need some ingredients.

Rather like baking a cake. If you follow the recipe correctly, then your cake should turn out the same each time. But we all know from experience that different types of oven give different results so my cake may not turn out the same as yours. But it will still be a cake!

Your main ingredients are *doing* it more, *learning* from the experience and then *changing/adjusting* it next time. You can apply this to any area of your life where you want to become more confident.

We have to do it more because until we make ourselves do it, we can't learn. For example, when a baby sees us walking, it wants to walk too but it doesn't succeed straightaway. It keeps getting up and falling down but with each attempt, the baby learns how to balance and adjust its posture little by little so that it is steadier next time. A baby doesn't know anything about failure so it doesn't give up trying. In fact, it takes most babies about 1000 hours of practise from the time they pull themselves upright to the time they can walk alone!

When I used to teach this course to the students at Capernwray International Bible College each year, I always asked the foreign students whether their English had quickly improved since arriving in the UK. They would all say it had. The reason for this is because they *had* to use it to get along with everyone else at the college.

When you have to do something you often realise that it's *not as hard as you feared* and the learning process speeds up.

At the moment, I'm trying to master eBay but I'm not succeeding because I don't go on-line enough to familiarise myself with the way it works. It all seems a bit daunting so I keep putting it off. But now I'm after some extra cash to buy a few bits and bobs for the house so I'm being forced to do it. Soon, all the mysteries of eBay will disappear and I'll sell all my unwanted items.

I open the course with an icebreaker to help everyone get to know each other. Not everyone welcomes this because they've had a miserable experience of it in the past so they are always pleasantly surprised to find that they actually enjoy this one (as I hope you did if you've done Session 1).

Things often *appear* scarier than they really are so just get on and *do* it anyway.

14

The research I've done tells us to:

Build confidence into our lives as a *daily* habit

And we can do that by taking:

A step-by-step approach, changing 1% by 1%

I've centred these 2 statements because that is the *method* you are going to use to build the confidence you need. (On the course, I even have a dance that goes with it!) This is the principle on which I get the most feedback and many women have conquered steep hills and mountains in their lives by using this tool.

You are aiming to **move forward little by little**.

There's nothing wrong with small increments; they are easy to control and often go unnoticed. Back in the 1970s, I took my car for its MOT and the mechanic told me it was pulling to the left so much, he was surprised I wasn't constantly hitting the curb. I knew he was right but I realised that over time, I had simply adjusted my wrist position to compensate for the extra pull. Someone else getting into the driving seat had picked up the fault straightaway. He went on to tell me that this is a common problem because the wheel alignment slips so slowly that you are unable to feel the change with each 500 miles or so.

Q. What have you slipped into without noticing? It may be affecting you in ways you haven't realised.

'We first make our habits, and then our habits make us'
John Dryden, Brainy Quotes

Tales

Up to the age of 30, I could eat whatever I liked without putting on weight. Of course, bad habits had formed (like a full packet of biscuits with my afternoon brew!) and I was slowly but surely piling on the pounds. Suddenly, I was no longer a puff of air but a lead weight. My clothes didn't feel comfy; you know the drill but if you don't, good for you. Rather than giving up the biscuits, I decided to cut out the sugar in my 10 daily cuppas. I took 2 teaspoons in each so that was a whopping 20 spoonfuls a day. It was fairly easy to get down to 1 teaspoon right away but I really struggled to reduce it any further. One of my friends said that if I could do without it for 3 weeks, my sugar addiction would be cured. Oh the misery of that 3 weeks; it was torture and it didn't even work! I was still missing my sugar fix so I decided to reduce it grain by grain and in 2 weeks, I managed to go down to ¾ of a teaspoon, then a ½ and finally, a ¼. In the end, even a scanty 3 grains mattered but I did it by educating my tongue bit by bit.

Small degrees of change are powerful.

Take the weather. If you're reading this in Britain, the chances are that it's cold, windy, or raining. (Don't be put off visiting us if not) When the temperature goes down to 1 or 2 degrees it feels cold but when it drops to zero, there are *visible* signs of frost and ice. That's a small reduction in temperature but it still produces a powerful and noticeable effect. The changes you are making may seem small and unnoticeable but they are still powerful.
I've seen free-divers who can dive deep into the ocean and then hold their breath for over 15 minutes! They achieve this level of fitness by increasing their lung capacity over time, little by little, second by second.

What stops us from making strides towards change?

I've got something of a tooth fetish and I love flossing and cleaning my teeth. My electric toothbrush is wonderful because it stops automatically after 2 minutes so I know I've done a proper job. One day when I was cleaning my teeth, my son James came into the bathroom to ask me something but said he would come back when I'd finished. He came back 5 minutes later but, to his astonishment, I was still cleaning away. And then I suddenly realised why it was taking so long; I was using an ordinary toothbrush! You see, I was in the *habit* of my brush stopping, not me stopping, so I was waiting for that to happen.

Our habits stop us from getting on with making changes so you must keep them in check. A large percentage of what we do each day is automatic and habitual. Get up; bathroom; breakfast; get dressed; go to work; same café or sandwich 3 times a week; same drinks; same route to work; same parking spot and so on.

Q. How many of you are having the same meals each week? I know we do, and it's hard to be different when your hubby only likes peas, carrots, potatoes, red meat, chicken and curry. (Do email me any recipe containing these ingredients).

Think about this perceptive comment on the subject of habit:
Habit is a self-imposed straitjacket of which the wearer is unaware.

(Arthur Koestler – author, journalist and intellectual)

If we aren't careful, what we do each day will stop us from doing anything different. I have important people in my life whose day-to-day existence is governed by *stale routines*. They are restricted and inflexible and this affects those around them who find it difficult to fit into their rigid schedules. They seem completely oblivious to the strain it puts on relationships. Unfortunately, they are locked into a comfort zone that has selfishness and sometimes fear, at its centre.

Some routine in our life is good and necessary but we *must* review what we do to ensure that it has not *passed its sell-by date*.

Romans 12v2 says do not conform any longer to the pattern of this world, but be transformed by the renewing of your mind. Then you will be able to test and approve what Gods will is – His good and pleasing will. (NIV)

One of my favourite stories is of a young newly-wedded girl. She was preparing a leg of lamb for her hubby and he saw her cut off the end off the bone and waste the meat. He asked why she done that and she explained that it was a family recipe handed down from her mum. When she subsequently asked her mum about it, she found out that she got the idea from her mum. So why do you think grandma did it? Actually, it was because it wouldn't fit into the roasting tin! You have to laugh at that don't you? But seriously, although it was *right* for grandma to do it that way *then*, it was no longer relevant. When I reviewed my out-of-date habits, I managed to reclaim about 10 hours a week over a 6-month period. This is how I did it:

MINDFULLY- thinking things on purpose

The best habit we can form is one where we ask ourselves:

What am I doing today? Is it current, relevant and effective?

When you've done this for a few days you will fall into *better routines that work for you*, your family and friends.

 Another tool I have tried successfully is the *Y Technique* from Japan. You ask yourself, 'W*hy* am I doing this?' When you get the answer, you ask, *'Why'* again of the answer to the question. Keep repeating the exercise until you get to the fifth *'Why'* (but you often get a result on the second or third) and, by then, you will have revealed the real *motive* behind what you are doing. Then you can ask yourself whether it is *still* important to do this, right now, at this time. We are driven by our motives (but I'm not going to cover that in this book).

An example of how it worked for me

I used to read a Saturday and Sunday newspaper. It started because my infant son woke up very early every day and it was something to pass the time between his naps. It was my little reward for the early starts and I really enjoyed all the weekend features. By the time I asked myself why I was doing this, my son was 10 years old but I had continued to have the papers delivered and because they weren't cheap, I felt that I had to read them from cover to cover! So what had started out as a reward, had now become a time-wasting chore that consumed my weekend. Realising this enabled me to free up my time to do other enjoyable things such as taking a day trip. I could buy a paper if I wanted to but I no longer felt that I had to. The power of the habit was broken.

When you have completed the *'Why'* exercise, use the information to make an informed decision about your routines and habits. Decide whether they are still right for you or if it's time to make some adjustments.

Aim to simplify your life

Q Can you think of anything you do without thinking about its relevance?

Patterns of thinking

When I travelled back south on the M6 motorway after speaking at various conferences, I would always be on the lookout for a deep groove in the tarmac around junction 34. At some point a lorry must have skidded on a hot day. If you hit the groove at speed, you were forced to travel in it until you could safely right yourself.
It was dangerous and very frightening so I learned to avoid it. (Fortunately, it has now been repaired).

Science shows that patterns of thinking that form *habits* become like deep grooves in our minds. We fall into them automatically and they are difficult to get out of just like the deep groove on the M6. Our habits are hard to break and there are many tips for changing them. (I have just read a great book, which I've included in the index). For instance, I've found that just missing something once can help you to see that you can live without it, even if you resume it right away. I want to give you this simple information that will form part of the formula for building confidence as a daily habit.

You have the power to change your thinking.

Did you take that in? I didn't realise that the power lies within me and maybe you didn't either.

Since researching Confidence Gym in 2004, there have been numerous publications about the workings of the mind. Dr Caroline Leaf, a cognitive neuroscientist, writes about epigenetics which is the study of our thoughts and how they affect specific places in the brain or body. We can't control 30% of our genetic make-up but that means we can control 70% by the choices we make. The research suggests that the whole body – what it feels and how it performs - is affected by our thoughts, be they positive or negative. Your life-style choices about diet, exercise, sleep, where you live, your social circle and so on, can cause chemical modifications around the genes (both good and bad ones) that will, over time, turn them on or off.

2Cor.10v5 says. We demolish arguments and every pretention that sets itself up against the knowledge of God, and WE TAKE CAPTIVE EVERY THOUGHT and make it obedient to Christ. (NIV) **So the power is in your hands!**

We see in the Bible that God gave Adam, the first man, the gift of free will but Adam chose to go his own way and disobey the God who had given him life (Genesis Chapter 3). Evil was introduced into what should have been a perfect world and, here we are thousands of years later, in a twisted society of self-gratification causing feelings of profound despair and hopelessness. We too have free will and the ability to choose - it's in our DNA – and we can use it *at will* for good and bad.

I heard about a World War 2 prisoner who refused to be beaten down by his cruel captors. His fellow prisoners asked him how he could remain cheerful when he was working knee-high in filth and eating barely enough to stay alive. He replied, 'Because my attitude is the one thing they can't control.' He got a kick from being in charge of his day-to-day drudgery and he was one of only a few to survive, a fact that he puts down to his attitude. The following quote sums it up really well:

Your attitude determines your altitude.

(Zig Ziglar – author and motivational speaker)

 **Q.** Can you rise above your circumstances like that?

Confidence is produced in the mind.

We need to know *how* the mind works. I've always been interested in science and although I got top marks in class tests, I still failed my 'O' Level. Some boy probably distracted me, but I'll come back to the power of distraction later.

When I used to check out the science section in my local bookshop, there were very few books on the mind and body but now in 2016, I am staggered at the massive choice. Over the years, I've studied many books for Confidence Gym and you will find these in the index for further study of your own.

The subject of confidence is quite complex but I now want to give you the basics so that you will be able to understand the things that drive you into decision making, for which there is always a consequence or action.

There are 2 parts to your mind: the conscious and subconscious.

The *conscious* mind is responsible for decision-making based on information received by your five senses.

The *subconscious* mind is responsible for automatic functions such as breathing, circulation and, most importantly, your nervous system **where feelings are created.** The subconscious cannot think or reason independently; it merely obeys the commands it receives from your conscious mind. Think of it this way: the *conscious mind* is the gardener planting seeds and the *subconscious mind* is the garden, or fertile soil, in which those seeds will germinate, grow and flourish.

So whatever thoughts are going through your conscious mind, the subconscious will automatically pick up on them and receive them as commands. For example, if you keep saying that you're tired, your subconscious will run a programme in your body to rest you so that you will start to *feel* tired. Go on, just start thinking of something you enjoy and it won't be long before you feel like doing it. All actions start with a thought.

Think of the conscious mind as a *captain* giving the *orders*. The subconscious mind is the *crew* which *acts* on those orders and steers you one way or the other. If you don't give good commands, then you'll end up stranded!

You are the captain of your soul.

 I used to watch a Channel 4 TV programme called *Panic Attack, which* helped to cure people of their phobias. There were some strange phobias such as clowns and buttons but they started off with something fairly common - spiders. Over the course of a few days,

people went from not even being able to look at a spider to actually holding one in their hand. I followed the programme's advice and techniques and my fear of spiders went down from 10 to 2. I still don't like it when one scuttles across my path but I can now grab a glass and a card to catch it and put it outside. The techniques focussed on bringing the fear out into the open and then issuing commands to the subconscious by repeatedly saying out loud, 'I am not frightened of spiders.' Spiders are beneficial because they help control insects, some of which carry disease. This knowledge enabled me to reframe how I *saw* spiders, as friends rather than enemies. The power of positive thinking, as opposed to negative thinking, can release people from their crippling phobias.

God did not design us to suffer from such anxiety disorders.

Science is also using neuro-linguistic programming (NLP) and cognitive behavioural therapy (CBT) to reprogramme the way people's minds work. Both of these techniques treat mental disorders by changing unhelpful thinking and behaviours.

When thoughts run through our nervous system (the subconscious mind), they are felt as *stress* or *elation*.

In my early thirties, I had still not conceived and because I had been experiencing abdominal pain, my GP thought I might have endometriosis, a condition of the womb that can affect fertility. This had to be investigated but when I went to the surgery to arrange my first hospital appointment, I found to my horror that my doctor had forgotten all about me and gone home! This was the final straw and I couldn't keep my emotions in check any longer; I just burst into floods of tears. I imagine they felt sorry for me so they made arrangements, there and then, for me to see a female doctor. She asked me lots of detailed questions about my general health and specific symptoms and then asked if I had ever heard of IBS (irritable bowel syndrome), which can also affect fertility. I did have abdominal pain but no obvious bowel problems. When she asked if I was suffering from any stress other than not being able to conceive, it suddenly

23

hit me that there was a bad atmosphere at work because a colleague had fallen out with me and another member of staff. She explained that stress directly affects the nervous system but the physical symptoms differ from one person to another. Some experience headaches, others are affected by their stomach, and some, like me, suffer with bowel pain. That night, I resolved to sort out the problem at work and the day after when I woke up, the ache had completely disappeared, never to return! This experience taught me that physical symptoms with no obvious physical cause are usually stress-related. Armed with this knowledge, I can now address the problem quickly.

When I was 8 years old, my father was very ill, pale and withdrawn for weeks on end and then, almost overnight, he was his old self again. Years later when I was completing a family medical history form, I asked my mum about dad's illness. She laughed and said he'd had diarrhoea for a while and, being something of a worrier, he'd convinced himself he was slowly dying! My mum rang our GP, not because she thought dad was really ill, but because she felt he was making himself ill because of what he *believed* about his condition. When dad arrived home from his doctor's appointment, he was positively elated – he wasn't dying after all! He just had to hear it from a professional to *believe* it.

The mind is everything. What you think and believe, you will become.

That's what today's research tells us and indeed, the Bible confirms it:

For as he thinks in his heart, so is he.

(Proverbs 23:7 New King James Version)

The medical profession trades on this by sometimes using placebos to encourage people to self-heal in minor ailments. They are deceived into thinking that they are taking drugs and the *belief* that they are receiving a pill to deal with the problem, enables them to overcome the illness.

24

Belief is powerful

Earlier, I talked about being unable to conceive. This went on for 12 years and in the summer of 1995 I was admitted to hospital for a medical procedure. The nurse who prepared me for theatre told me that after the procedure, I would have a very good chance of getting pregnant within the next 3 months. She had seen many cases where this had happened - something inside me grabbed on to that fact and gave me real hope. And guess what, two months later I was pregnant. I'm sure that my *belief* was important but sadly, that pregnancy didn't go to full term. I was utterly devastated and confused but I sensed God telling me that I would be pregnant again before the end of the year. This time the *belief* factor was sky high and sure enough, on December 17th 1995, James Anthony Ainsworth was conceived!

Many of our habits are connected with our beliefs.

For example, my preferred drink is tea but, to me, it only tastes good when it's served in a china teacup. I'm a nightmare when I go to friends' houses because if they only have mugs, I have to drink coffee which I don't really enjoy.

You see, beliefs can *create* work and they can also *limit* you.

Jesus used people's beliefs to heal them. Interestingly, he couldn't perform any miracles in his home town. Why not? Because they didn't *believe* he was who people said he was. To them, he was just an ordinary local boy, the carpenter's son - nobody special. Mary was healed after just touching His cloak she had such faith Mathew chapter 9 v21 & 22 tells us.

Beliefs are also shaped by our experiences, becoming useful. The fire will burn you, which is rational. Jumping under the table when it thunders, irrational and harmful. This can stop you doing things. I knew a lady who had a bad experience swallowing a tablet. It created difficulties swallowing any more for years, at least 15, before she got treatment for it. I got

25

it into my head that the vibrations from my electric toothbrush might set off a miscarriage when I was pregnant. I didn't take any chances and used a normal brush until he was born. (I know; it seems silly)

Externals affect our minds

As I was researching Confidence Gym, I came across some research undertaken by Professor Richard Wiseman. He conducted an experiment using groups of people who were asked to construct sentences with a variety of words, some positive and some negative. After completing the task, each person handed in their work to a receptionist who had been primed to ignore them.

The results of the experiment revealed that those who had constructed sentences with positive words such as love, patience, kindness, honour, grace etc. were more patient than those using negative words like hatred, kill, cruelty, stab etc. One lady waited patiently for over 5 minutes before the receptionist acknowledged her whereas one man started to show his impatience after only 30 seconds. You'll have worked out which group each of them came from!

When the experiment was repeated using words associated with old age, it was observed that the participants actually walked out slower than they had walked in.

So we must be very careful what we *watch, read* and *listen* to. Even though we may not be aware of it, it *does* affect us.

That's why it is so important to read your Bible every day or, if you are not a Christian, get some positive, uplifting words into your day. (There is a highly rated, free iTunes app called *Inspirational and Motivational Quotes – Daily Quote of the Day*).

Psalm 119 v 105. Your word is a lamp for my feet and a light on my path. (NIV)

For 10 years, I hardly did any daily Bible reading. I was in church leadership, going on with God, so I didn't think I needed it. I might not have been reading my Bible every day but I <u>was</u> watching TV. What I didn't realise was that some of the programmes I was watching can have a direct effect on my subconscious. Programmes that send out the wrong messages e.g. having an affair can be good for your marriage; it's ok to gossip and tell lies; it's fine to make yourself your number 1 priority etc., can seriously warp our thinking and behaviour. Newspapers with their accounts of war, violence and despair can make you anxious and suspicious of everything and everybody around you. These thoughts and fears creep up on you slowly but they can lead to serious disorders and phobias such as anorexia, agoraphobia etc.

Some of you probably think you've got a bad memory and that if you read the Bible, you'd never remember it. You can't remember every meal you've ever eaten but they've all contributed to your health and well-being. And so it is with the Bible. The words go in and quietly build you up. Then when you've got problems or worries, you'll find that the words and right kind of wisdom will come back to you.

Barriers to building confidence

1. Building confidence IS uncomfortable

If you've been on Session 1, you may remember that half way through I ask you to go and sit on another table with people you don't know. Most people don't like it, but you have to *expect* every change you make to sometimes be a bit of trouble. It's all part of the transition.

It *is* going to *feel* and look different when you *try* to make any change but you do *get used* to it quickly, especially if your change is 1% by 1%. Do this little exercise with me. Clasp your hands together with your thumbs crossed. That probably feels quite comfortable and familiar to you but now, without opening your hands, change your thumbs over. 75% of you will be thinking it doesn't feel quite right but if you cross your thumbs back to their original position, you'll immediately feel comfortable again. If you keep repeating this exercise, you will find that each time you do it, the change doesn't seem as bad as it did the first time. And the more you do it, the less noticeable it becomes.

 In 1990 my mum's Servis twin tub washing machine finally gave up the ghost. She was horrified when the engineer suggested she should upgrade to a front loader. The twin tub was messy to use, hard work and time consuming but that's what she was *used* to. I drove all over Lancashire trying to find a twin tub but to no avail so in the end, my mum had to concede defeat and have a new front loader. After 2 weeks of getting used to it, she was converted and on my next visit home, she was full of praise for its efficiency and ease of use; she couldn't think why she hadn't bought one sooner! So change isn't always for the worse, it's just the *thought* of it that scares us. And when we are put in the position of being *forced* to change, we often find that *it's not as bad as we feared.* Indeed, I always laugh when people in the seminar have secured a better seat.

28

2. We have a negative default setting

One morning, just as my husband Tony was leaving for work, we had a tiff about how untidy the place was becoming. Afterwards, he rang to say that he'd forgotten to take his mobile phone (probably because of the argument) and asked me to listen out for it to pick up any important business calls.

Later on that day as I took a break from the housework for a cuppa, I noticed that I had a voicemail. I couldn't make out exactly what was being said but I could hear the person shouting and I could tell they were pretty mad at someone. This was so exciting but who on earth was it?! And then I heard the words, 'Well that should keep yer trap shut Tony!' Yes, you've guessed – it was me!

I had put Tony's phone in my pocket, and somehow I had clicked on the redial button, which just happened to connect to my number. Hence, my conversation with him had been recorded! What shocked me was that I had no idea of the *foul* mood I was in. It's one thing for somebody to tell you so but it's quite another to hear the recorded evidence! I was ashamed of my negative behaviour and attitude.

Modern psychology confirms it, giving an evolutionary twist to the fact. Saying we became unexpectant as hunter-gatherers as it helped to stem the disappointment if nothing was caught to eat that day.

In the Bible, Genesis Chapter 3 tells us that we have fallen from the perfect beings God created us to be and, as Adam and Eve listened to the serpent rather than God, negativity entered our lives – Satan (disguised as the serpent) is the father of negativity.

In my last house, there was a central heating timer which you could programme to set the times when you wanted the water and heating to come on and go off. But it was a real bind whenever there was a power cut because the timer would automatically default to the manufacturer's original setting of 12 noon. That's what we have become like from the start of the fall of man.

Try this out. Think about the day you've had and it won't be long before some negative thoughts enter your mind. Your hair wasn't right, you had a big spot, the train was late etc., etc. We tend to look for, and dwell upon, the negative rather than the positive, and we don't *recognise* it when it's happening. We tell ourselves that we are stupid, useless and hopeless and because what we say goes down deep on the inside, we then start to *feel* and *believe* that we really are stupid, useless and hopeless. This erodes our self-esteem.

If you had a lodger in your house who constantly found fault, you would soon kick them out. But we allow our negative thoughts to take up permanent residence little realising what damage they will do. We entertain thoughts like a juggler, throwing them up and down in front of us instead of throwing them away.

I know a lady who is rather like a jukebox of negativity. The minute you touch on *any* subject, she automatically selects and plays the negativity record; nothing and no one escapes her negative spin. The time when someone did this or that to her; the time when someone ignored her; the time when someone spoke sharply to her - you get the picture! She wonders why people avoid her and why she feels lonely and depressed much of the time. The truth is that her negativity is holding her captive. In Session 3 on Stress Busting, I will explain why it is so bad for you to keep recalling hurtful experiences.

 I was in the gym getting dressed after a swim and overheard a conversation. One woman was telling the other about her father's forthcoming operation for prostate cancer. The woman listening said that her uncle had died following the very same operation. What a thoughtless response. Sometimes we need someone to be there for us, not to fix anything or do anything in particular, but just so that we feel

supported and cared for. We should think before we speak. **Negativity crushes confidence!**

You have to replace these negative thoughts with positive ones in order to *lay down a foundation* that will enable you to succeed, not fail. So here's a technique I picked up from Stephen Matthew of Life Church, Bradford that really does work.

 **The formula is *recognise, refuse, replace*.**

1. *Recognise* a negative thought right away. It takes time for this to develop but the more you practice by *examining* each thought, the easier it becomes.

2. *Exercise power* over that thought **refusing** it in its tracks from becoming an action of worry or creating a different path for your life. Our thought life can be likened to waiting at a train station. Not every train that stops is going in the direction you want. Giving in to a negative thought is like getting on the first train to arrive at your platform without knowing where it's going. I once got on the wrong train and it created no end of problems. Now, I check the train as it arrives and make sure it's going to get me where I want to go.

3. **Replace** the negative thought with a positive one. Start noticing the good things people say about you, repeat them in your mind and then file them away in readiness to use like a weapon, when the negative thoughts come.

 I learned this principle of *recognise, refuse, replace* in 2007 and got a chance to put it into practice right away. I was asked to speak at a conference in Kendal, Cumbria where the organiser had arranged to have 2 massive TV screens at either side of the stage to enable those at the back to see. I thought I'd better make an effort to look good!

I don't usually wear much makeup but the year before along with some girlfriends, I made a spoof film to advertise our *Inspired Conference* in Lancashire. We were *Charlie's Angels* (a popular 1970s TV detective series) on a mission to put the event together (check my website to see if I've uploaded it). I played the part of the glamorous Kelly and my friends, who were all bang up to date with the latest trends, put a lime green eye shadow on me and a foundation that had a slight sparkle to it. Because I wasn't used to wearing makeup, it felt rather strange and I wondered if I looked like a clown! I was so reassured when they said I looked amazing and it really built my confidence.

On the morning of the Kendal conference, I had all my new makeup laid out ready to glam up. But suddenly a rush of fear hit me accompanied by a voice in my head saying that I was going to look over the top and ridiculous with all that stuff on. I sat looking at myself in the mirror wondering what to do and then it came to me that this was a negative thought; I had *recognised* it. Then I *refused* it by saying to myself, 'I'm not having that!' I *replaced* the negative thought with a positive one by recalling the number of people who had told me how attractive I looked with that style of makeup.

Feeling more confident, I applied my makeup and headed off for the conference. The guest speaker from Canada shook my hand warmly and said, 'Wow, your facial make up is beautiful. What foundation are you wearing?' If I ever needed a confirmation, it was right there and then. God always knows what we need and He always delivers. And the more I used the technique, the more second nature it became, sweeping away doubt and worry every time.

Laying a foundation to succeed

Another effective method is to look at the areas of your life that you are at odds with and make a *plan of action.*

32

The aim is to diminish as much negativity as possible. If you learn to recognise that every time you are with ……. (You fill in the name), you always end up gossiping, criticising, or judging someone else, then don't spend as much time with them. This can be a painful and difficult choice, particularly if it is a close friend or family member, but it is worth it in the long run.

If you really cannot limit contact, say to yourself before you meet up, 'I am *not* going to gossip' for example. By doing this, you will be more alert and aware when the conversation does turn to gossip. You will then be able to deflect it by changing the subject or confronting the other person about what they are saying.

Doing all this takes time and effort but when we work at something, we always get results. We can rely on some Bible verses here.

- **We demolish arguments and every pretension that sets itself up against the knowledge of God, and we take captive every thought to make it obedient to Christ.**

(2 Corinthians 10:5 New International Version)

So how do you make something obedient? You speak to it! That's exactly what we've been learning about.

- **Whatever is true, whatever is noble, whatever is right, whatever is pure, whatever is lovely, whatever is admirable – if anything is excellent or praiseworthy – think about such things.**

(Philippians 4:8 NIV)

Focus on positive and uplifting things. Take control of your thinking.

- **Think about the things of heaven, not the things of earth.**

(Colossians 3:2 New Living Translation)

Banish negative thinking. Speak words of affirmation to yourself each day.

3. Fear of failure

I could list a whole page of people who didn't succeed on their first attempt but that didn't make them give up. Thomas Edison was a prolific inventor and businessman. He invented the electric light bulb, the motion picture camera and many other devices that still impact today in the 21st century. He did thousands of experiments and those that didn't work gave him feedback for future attempts. In Edison's words, *'I have not failed. I've just found 10,000 ways that won't work.'*

Similarly, J K Rowling, the Harry Potter author, received many rejection letters before her books were published. Margaret Thatcher, our Prime Minister from 1979 to 1990, made numerous attempts to enter politics before finally being elected as MP for Finchley in 1959. Each time she lost, she saw it as an opportunity to learn from the experience and gain ground and confidence for the next attempt. She went on to become Europe's first woman prime minister and, at the time of her resignation, Britain's longest continuously serving prime minister since 1827.

What these people have in common is that they *kept on going on.* They kept *doing* and *changing* - the formula to building confidence. A formula that you can apply too.

Again, in Edison's words, *'Many of life's failures are people who did not realise how close they were to success when they gave up.'*

Earlier, I mentioned that a baby repeatedly gets up, trying to balance. The baby *keeps on going on* because it doesn't know the concept of failure, a response that

34

we learn subconsciously from the world around us. Babies just *keep on keeping on* regardless of how many times they fall down. The falling down is part of the process, nothing to get hung-up about.

4. Fear of what people think (embarrassment)

When it comes to self-esteem, this is one that can stop us in our tracks. In 1998, I was getting ready to go to Brownies. I was preparing a stew for the evening meal when I realised that I'd run out of gravy browning. No problem – I could pop to the local shop. As I stepped out of the door, purse in hand, an *unfamiliar* feeling of dread came over me. You see, my hair was pinned up in rollers! When I lived at my old house, I worked full-time and didn't really get to know anyone so nipping out to the shop in my slippers and rollers was no problem. People didn't know me so it didn't matter what they thought of me.

But things were completely different now. I was living in a new house in a busy village. As a young mum, I'd got involved with toddler groups and Brownies and I knew quite a lot of people. I couldn't be seen out in public in my rollers could I? What would people think?! What would they say about me! When people know us, we do care what they think; it matters to us.

I took half of my rollers out and slapped on a hat to disguise the rest. I was so annoyed. The truth is people might have noticed my rollers and had a good laugh, or even a critical thought, but so what? They would soon forget all about it because it wasn't in the least important. It was me making it a big deal!

Many of us like to dress in a way that expresses our inner fashionista so, on impulse, you buy a beautiful bright pink polka dot t-shirt. You have no sooner got it home than the doubts start to creep in. It's too bright; I'll stand out too much; I'm too old for that style; it draws attention to my boobs and so on. We've all been there haven't we? So once again, we allow the fear of embarrassment to steal our joy.

35

At a conference, my friend and I were getting changed for the Gala Dinner. She was frantically searching her suitcase for a pair of socks so I asked her why she couldn't wear the ones that were right by the side of her bag. I laughed out loud when she said it was because they didn't match. She was going to be wearing trousers so who on earth was going to see them! Did she think the sock police were on patrol? She laughed her head off at her silliness.

Here's the news on this one. People don't give a rip! They aren't thinking about *you* that much. Here's a little ditty I heard and it's so true.

When you're 18 you're worried what people think of you.
When you're 40 you don't care what people think of you.
When you're 60 you realise that no one was thinking about you anyway!

People may notice what you're wearing and have an opinion about it but it'll be forgotten in an instant when they move on to talking about something, or somebody, else.

How **you** *think* is reflected in what you say or expect of others. The Bible says:

For as he thinks in his heart, so is he.

(Proverbs 23:7 New King James Version)

Think on this and it let it challenge your thought life.

We don't see the world as it is - we see it as we are.

I know an elderly lady who is always fussing about what should she wear. I said she should wear what she wanted but then she confessed that it really mattered to her what others thought about her clothes. I was quite shocked when she then went on to admit that she makes a judgement about other people on the basis of what they are wearing. I suddenly realised that *what is important to you, you will look for in others*.

My husband likes to buy top-quality shoes so he invariably takes note of other people's shoes - it's important to him. I never even look down! Much to his annoyance, I'll wear anything that's comfy regardless of whether it matches my outfit. He respects someone who takes time and care over their shoes because in his experience, such people tend to take time and care with the other small details in their life thus making for a good friendship.

 This came home to me when I gave a friend a lift to a conference. I was quite annoyed that she didn't offer to contribute to the petrol costs as I would have done had I been given a lift. She wasn't mean, she was known for her generosity. As I fumed about it, I realised that I was putting what *I* would do onto her. In fact, if she gave anyone a lift she *never* expected help with the petrol – she saw it as a gift. A motive adjustment was obviously needed for me!

It will help you enormously to realise that others are not like you. What yo*u expect of others often reveals more about you and your judgements than it does about them.*

Try putting this principle into practise and you will find things out *about yourself* that you can take charge over.

And finally. Relax in the knowledge that you are *not* a celebrity 24/7. Make a fuss about your appearance when it matters – first dates, job interviews and such like. If you're ever lucky enough to attend a red carpet event, you can make as much fuss as you like!

5. Attitude is everything

We need to look at life differently by changing our attitudes 1% by 1%. This will build our self-esteem slowly but surely.

I was in a Girl Guiding training session and we were asked to do some kirigami (a variation of origami). You fold a piece of paper this way and that, make some cuts and hey presto, you get a really cool shape when you unfold the paper. The girl next to me said she had done kirigami before but always got it wrong which made me think it must be really difficult. There were 8 of us on the table and we all followed the instructions to the letter. When we opened our papers, 7 of us had correctly cut out the Brownie Guide trefoil emblem. Guess who had done it wrong. *In her head, she was beaten before she even started.*

The task wasn't that difficult but her negativity had spread to me and almost put me off trying the exercise in case I looked foolish!

Having the right attitude will *decrease stress* in your life.

When I became a Christian, one of the things that bugged me intensely was when people abbreviated Christmas to Xmas. I learned this from other Christians who told me it was taking the Christ out of Christmas. That's true but getting annoyed about it only causes *you* grief, not the people doing it. One Christmas, I was giving a friend earache about it and she told me I really needed to change my attitude! She said that instead of letting the word Xmas wind me up, I should *use* it to remind myself of the cross that Jesus died on to save me and then treat it as a kiss to confirm how much he loves me. I was taken aback at her wisdom but she persuaded me that it was possible to turn a negative feeling into something positive that would work for me. I knew it wouldn't be easy or comfortable to completely reverse my way of thinking but eventually, the *more* I replaced the negative thought with a positive one, the better I felt. Now, it doesn't bother me at all. That's *me* in control of my feelings not what I *see* on Christmas cards.

I used to hate housework but by using this *change of attitude* technique, I now enjoy it. How can that be I hear you cry?! About 7 years ago, in the absence of anything better on the box, I watched a TV programme hosted by Anthea Turner called *How to be a Perfect Housewife*. She took 2 women who were hopeless with household chores and showed them her top tips for cleaning, organising and entertaining. To my amazement, I was hooked after 1 episode especially when she demonstrated how to turn a towel into a turtle for the bottom of the guest bed! I hadn't realised that housework could be so creative. I started to use the tips, rearranging my bed linen into sets then popping them into a pillowcase and folding all my family's t-shirts in a jiffy. I was decreasing the time I needed to sort out my usual mess and having fun at the same time, patting myself on the back at a job well done.

You see, keeping the house nice is a service for your family. Its love disguised.

My husband Tony's love language is a tidy house and I didn't speak it very well! I wasn't meeting his need so there were frequent arguments about it. But after watching Anthea and adopting her ideas, I got so enthused that I put together a *Top Ten Tips* DVD for one of our conferences. Tony filmed me and some friends demonstrating them all in a *Stepford Wives* way. It was hilarious. (Check out my website as I may have a link to watch it by the time this is published).

I realised that **changing your attitude to anything** *is possible* and rewarding.

Change comes before transformation and that change can take time, like the pupae stage of a butterfly. It's an investment in you.

39

Think of things you can't do or things you don't like. *Ask* why you feel that way and whether that feeling is still relevant, *Change* your attitude bit by bit. After all, housework has to be done so you might as well enjoy it.

6. Switch a negative thought with a distraction

I was loading the dishwasher one day and talking away to myself. Actually, I was having an imaginary argument with someone who often annoyed me. You know what it's like; you think of something really witty and clever which would have shut them up if only you'd been quick enough to think of it at the time! Or you find yourself rehearsing what you'll say the next time they bug you. I will explain in my stress-busting section why it's not healthy to do this too often!

All of a sudden, one of my favourite records came on the radio. Now those of you who have been on the course will know my famous embarrassing story about dancing. (It may also be on the website.) I just can't help myself. Wherever I am, I've just got to start grooving and jiving, twisting and turning with an occasional leap here and there especially if it's Barbra Streisand's *Evergreen*. I stepped away from my argument to dance for a while. When the record finished, I tried to turn my mind back to the spat that I'd been dwelling on but for the life of me, I couldn't even remember what it was about. It had gone from my mind. It suddenly dawned on me how my dancing had been a helpful *distraction* in getting rid of the hurt I was feeling. I resolved to see how I could apply this in my life over the next few months.

Every time I had a thought that wasn't in line with something valuable and worthwhile in my life, I chose to think about something else, turned the radio on or started a shopping list - anything to prevent the irritating thought from *flourishing*. I found myself having less and less imaginary conversations and worrying about stuff that would probably never happen. I'll be sharing how to deal with worries in a very practical and efficient way later on.

There's something else I also discovered about the power of distraction. You can even *override* bodily functions!

On Wednesday mornings after dropping James at school, I would head off for a swim. As it was a 50-minute journey, I always went to the loo before setting off but on this particular day I forgot. I also got stuck in a traffic jam so by the time I arrived at the gym I was desperate to go and holding myself like a small child! I staggered into the gym, fumbling to find my card. All of a sudden, I saw a notice saying that the Spa would be closed that day. Some rude words went through my mind; I was so cross as I was really looking forward to my 10-minute sauna. Why, oh why, did they always have to do this cleaning routine on a Wednesday? I caught the manager's attention and complained at some length. Having got my irritation out of my system, I set off for the changing room and suddenly realised that my urge to wee had completely disappeared. That's amazing I thought. I just got distracted and was able to suppress my bladder!

On one occasion at church, my friend Kathy sat down behind me and as I turned round to speak to her, I could see that she didn't look well. I began to ask what was troubling her and then another friend, Ruth, joined me to comfort her. Ruth was crouching down on the floor and someone brushed past knocking her off her feet and onto her bottom, legs high in the air. She looked hilarious and the 3 of us just couldn't stop laughing. When I looked at Kathy again, her face had completely changed. When I asked her how she was feeling she replied, 'Absolutely marvelous!' Laughing out loud had distracted her and dispelled her negative mood.

Later, I'll be sharing how laughter is an incredible tool in our armory.

Like everything I've shared, you have to work hard initially with these techniques and tools but the more you do them, the more they become *second nature*.

41

You'll remember when you started to drive, how hard it was getting all the different manoeuvres into your head and then performing them simultaneously. It took concentration and *will* to master but now you don't give it a thought, you do it *automatically*. And that's exactly what will happen when you persevere with these techniques and tools.

OK, you've taken a lot in. Go & grab a brew & let it all sink in.

- **Building confidence needs to be done as a daily habit.**

- **Check your habits.**

- **Make small changes.**

- **Confidence is produced in the mind.**

- **Belief is powerful.**

- **Get rid of negative thinking.**

- **Recognise, refuse, replace.**

- **Building confidence is uncomfortable.**

- **Lay a foundation to succeed.**

- **It's feedback, not failure.**

- **No one is thinking about you that much.**

- **Attitude determines altitude.**

- **Use distraction to your advantage.**

1

Building Self-Esteem

After you have absorbed everything that I've shared in the first section of the book, we now have a foundation on which to build.

I have already mentioned that **YOU** have the power to choose. You must now *use* that power to **choose** good things to believe about yourself. **In other words, be a 5%er**.

There are many biblical principles concerned with building up your self-worth. All too often, we dismiss ourselves as being unworthy. When we receive a compliment about a nice dress we are wearing, why do we say we got it second-hand or that we bought it from a really cheap shop? We don't need to apologise or make excuses; we have the *right* to look good and spend money on ourselves. After all, as the advert says, 'We're worth it.'

If we look to the Bible, that's certainly true. God thinks we are wonderful but this truth isn't fully understood and appreciated; this lies at the root of our **feelings** of unworthiness. Early on in my seminars, I discovered that we do not like talking about our good qualities because we have been conditioned to see it as pride. We can think of a dozen faults right away but not our positive attributes.

As I put my first Confidence Gym session together, I had learned from various TV programmes and books, that if you want to build yourself up, you have to love yourself. When Jesus was asked which command in God's law was the most important, He replied:

> *Love the Lord your God with all your heart and with all your soul and with all your mind. This is the first and greatest commandment. And the second is like it: Love your neighbour as yourself.*

(Matthew 22:37-39 New International Version)

It isn't pride but rather, it is accepting that you are God's workmanship and that you are made in His likeness.

44

Not believing what He says about you is like saying, 'You got it wrong God.'

At my first ever session, I was amazed how difficult the women found it to compliment themselves. Using a principle, I had seen on a life-coaching programme, I asked them to write down on post-it notes, 10 good things about themselves. The aim was to identify and celebrate these things and get them deep down in the subconscious so that they would be **less self-critical** and **more self-compassionate**. I could see by the anguished looks on their faces that they were struggling to complete the task even though it was private and not to be shared. At subsequent sessions, I reduced it to 6 and then finally to 3 because experience has shown me that most women are comfortable with this and can complete it successfully.

At the same time, I also ask them to write down 1 good thing about someone in the room and go and post it on them. There is never any problem with this task so why is it so much easier to think of something positive about someone else rather than ourselves? It's because of the mindset we have developed which is often a learned experience from childhood.

The Bible says that words have 'the power of life and death' (Proverbs 18:21 New International Version). The childhood saying 'sticks and stones may break my bones but names will never hurt me' is nonsense! The American singer and drummer Karen Carpenter, died at the age of 32 of heart failure caused by complications related to her eating disorder, anorexia nervosa. It is thought that the comments of an insensitive news reporter, who described her as chubby in her teens, damaged her self-image and reinforced her belief that she was overweight. It was the start of 17 years of anguish and wrong-thinking. I cried when I first heard that story because it was so tragically unnecessary.

This world is full of lies, particularly in the media. How you must look; how it's OK to behave just as you like; if it feels good, do it; you're not loved if your partner isn't acting in this way or that, and so on. It's in many of the TV programmes you watch, going in subconsciously and making you *feel* inadequate, unloved and unworthy. That's why you **must** be on your guard against what you *see* and *read*.

It is **essential** to get God's opinion of you. Feed your soul with His word and let it go deep down on the inside. Reading your Bible everyday **will** enable you to combat what this world throws at you. When you start to see yourself as God sees you, then you will bloom. But you've got to believe it. And the best way of achieving this belief is to **repeat it out loud.** At the end of this session, you will find a list of things that God thinks about you.

 Try this exercise yourself now. Get some post-it notes and write down a minimum of 3 things; you could even try for 6.

Your *daily* exercise for 2 weeks is to repeat them all out loud several times every day, like a mantra. So put up your post-it notes in places you will visit each day (the biscuit tin!) and then, as you come across each good quality, **repeat it out loud 10 times**. I didn't understand why this works until I came across the research by Dr Joseph Murphy in his book *The Power of Your Subconscious Mind*. Then it all made sense. The positive statement is received as an instruction by the subconscious mind and you start to *feel* better about yourself.

As Confidence Gym developed, I added in another little exercise. It involves each lady closing her eyes, giving herself a big hug and saying the words, 'I like myself' 3 or 4 times. I noticed that about 10% of the ladies just couldn't do it. The truth is they didn't actually like themselves, never mind love themselves, and the conversations I had with them afterwards, confirmed that this was indeed the case. You may have heard it said that you can only give out what you've got and whilst I don't think that's absolutely true, I firmly believe you are more effective at showing real love to others if you are a big fan of yourself.

 **Q Can you close your eyes and hug yourself?**

Then say, 'I *like* myself' and then move on to say, 'I *love* myself.' If you struggle to do this, then you could be one of the 10% who don't actually like themselves. *That's your cue to do something about it.*

Another exercise I do to help overcome negative mindsets is developed from this Albert Einstein quote:

> '*Your imagination is your preview of life's coming attractions.*'

So I do a meditation on visualising yourself being happy or, for those who are Christians, being in God's hands. As I lead the ladies through this 2-minute daydream, you should see the smiles on the faces of those who are imagining what I say. Again, you need to do it **daily** to get the full effect. You can do it on your own. Just make up a little story, learn it well and then run through it in your mind. If you say you are no good at making up stories, I don't believe you. Let me remind you of this old chestnut - 'My new dress was only 10 pence at the charity shop darling!'

Later on in the book, I'll explain the significance of our imagination and how it connects to our nervous system.

It's important that we get along with ourselves by not being critical of what we *do, think* or *give in* to. After all, we spend all day with ourselves - you can't get away for a rest can you?! So let's enjoy who God has made us to be. If you didn't do it earlier, start making a list now of your best qualities and put that list up where you can see it. Start a <u>daily habit</u> of speaking these qualities out loud. If you really are struggling to think of things, then ask those who know you best.

REMEMBER - IF YOU DON'T DO IT, NOTHING CHANGES

That leads me to one of the most exciting things I've discovered.

Building up others will increase YOUR self-esteem!

You'll have heard the worldly expression '*What goes around comes around*' and we often say it when we want to see someone get their comeuppance. Well it's also true in the <u>positive</u>, not just the negative. The Bible says, 'A man reaps what he sows.' (Galatians 6:7 New International Version). Some of the research I have done suggests that it will come back to you as a boomerang does, much harder than it was thrown. That's double for your trouble and, in my experience, it's true.

We should be in the business of adding value to others. Romans 15 verse 2 talks about building up our neighbours for their good. It seems when we do we get a payback.

I've always been generous with my compliments. I don't find it hard, they just burst from me. I have been told that I am a great encourager. Don't assume that good-looking girls know it and don't need to hear it. I've often found it to be the opposite. We can all benefit from a good word said, *adding* it to our collection. **Start noting** any time someone says something nice to you and file it away for this exercise of building your self-esteem. Write it on a post-it note. By the way, once the 2 weeks of shouting good things are up, you then have the challenge of writing more things to acknowledge and shouting them out for the next 2 weeks. Make sure it's not in a public place though!

There is a lovely effect that you can feel right away as you see others give out care and attention. It's called the Elevation Effect. You can do yourself a lot of good by choosing to watch programmes where enjoyable, uplifting things happen to people e.g. Secret Millionaire, Noel's Christmas Presents and Surprise Surprise. These are all British TV shows that build people up and shower them with love and affection.

They also reunite people with long-lost relatives. The same goes for makeover shows. When you see happy times, it rubs off on *you*.

Giving encouragement is like giving a pint of blood; you can afford to part with it and it can give a new lease of life to someone else. In the Bible, the apostle Paul talks about his friend Onesiphorus in 2 Timothy. When Paul was in prison in Rome, many of his friends abandoned him but Onesiphorus stepped up and was faithful to him. He made the difficult journey to Rome and searched long and hard to find Paul so that he could bring him cheer, refreshment and restore joy to his soul. He was the wind beneath Paul's wings. The gift of friendship is an awesome tool.

Thing is, I don't see it being used to its full extent in today's world.

Q Have you ever chased anybody down to give him or her a lift up?

So how do we do it then?
- Attune yourself to notice the positive in people.
- Be liberal with praise.
- Compliment frequently, sincerely and publically.
- Use someone's first name as often as you can. I love it when one of my friends uses my name every three or four sentences because it makes me feel special. Notice how good you feel when people do it to you.
- Notice their hobbies and interests and if there's an article or programme that would be of interest, save it for them or send them an email link, text or phone to let them know.

All these little things *show* that you care.

1 Thess 5 v11. Therefore, encourage one another and build each other up. (NIV)

Thanks a lot!

 *Saying thank you can have such an amazing effect on people.*

For some reason again, this is a natural trait in my personality and I am quick to notice and appreciate others that practise it.

It's so simple yet people don't think of it.

During my 9 years in Brownies, I must have had 70 girls under my guidance but I can count on 2 hands the mums who thought to say thank you at the end of their daughters' Brownie experience.

We all want to be valued

Whenever we received a little card, a box of chocolates or a plant, we would *feel* fantastic that someone appreciated all the time and effort we had given to the girls. It's not hard is it so why don't more people think to do it?

 **Q** When did you last make the effort to thank someone?

 At my gym, the changing rooms are always spotless and fresh. One day, I saw one of the girls and thanked her for doing such a good job and told her that it was one of the main reasons I stayed a member. I could tell she was really thrilled to hear that her role, albeit not a very glamorous one, was vitally important in the success of the gym. She also went on to say that no one had ever taken the time to tell her that and point out how important her contribution was. She could now take pride in her job.

A few words only take seconds but their impact can last for days and months.

50

I have also used this powerful tool of thanking someone to change their behaviour towards me.

 As part of my work, I had to attend a monthly planning meeting. This was always difficult for me because it was obvious that the secretary didn't like me. Whenever I made a suggestion, it was often pooh-poohed or ignored and there was no attempt to include me. Unfortunately, this person was also very influential so others copied her attitude towards me and I often went home feeling disheartened and unappreciated. When I prayed about this, I felt the Lord saying, *'Thank her for her work, **she** is underappreciated.'* I didn't like the thought of that I can tell you, but I trusted what I felt and began to think what I could do. At the next meeting, I overheard her say she was starving because she had come straight from another job to take the minutes at ours. I asked her about this and soon I had my reason. I wrote a short letter thanking her for the sacrifice she makes each month and for sending out really professional minutes to us all the very next day. At the next meeting, her attitude was quite different. She beamed at me as I came in and thanked me for acknowledging her work. During that day's discussions, I was included, my opinions were sought and my comments and suggestions were considered. The atmosphere of the meeting was changed and the chemistry much better for me. From then on, we became friends and I was able to invite her to many events. All that from a simple note. I have thanked other people who I haven't felt deserved it because of their attitude towards me but I've pressed on and seen dramatic changes, which benefited **me,** not just them.

 Try it. Who could you thank for all their hard work? I can promise you it will make them feel amazing and special.

At the end of Confidence Gym, I have a 'Being Thankful' session where I've contacted people in advance and asked them to write a note to someone present that they

51

would be willing to read out. It's always a very powerful moment and lots of tears flow all around the room as the ladies see the effect of a few words of thanks and encouragement. I have just broken off from writing this to write to someone else that I know will be lifted by a word of encouragement. It will be fuel in his tank as he drives kindness towards others.

Smiling brings acceptance

Another way we can increase self-esteem in others and ourselves is to simply smile. In Session 4, I've got a whole section about the importance of laughter in our lives, but for now I want to stress the impact of moving a few facial muscles.

 I was working on a film set chaperoning my then 14-year old son, James who is an actor. After the first week, people kept asking me if I was all right. I always replied, 'Yes of course! I'm fine.' One lady who always spoke her mind then said, 'Well, you just look miserable that's all!' Charming! After what she said had sunk in, I turned to James and asked, 'Do I?' and to my horror he said, 'Well now I think about it mum, you do look fed up most of the time!' I felt terrible.

I was shocked to learn that my resting face looks miserable!

I had no idea I came across like that. I felt happy on the inside but it didn't show on the outside in my facial *expression*. Whenever I pass a mirror, I always tend to smile as a habit and so I'm not seeing what everyone else is. Infact every morning, I look in the bathroom mirror and say, 'lookin' good kid!' I do this no matter what my bed-head looks like. It's a good habit and I always end up smiling at this statement alone because not many of us look good when we've just got out of bed!

In our brains, there is a section that responds to a smile. It's a 'mirror neuron' meaning that if you smile at people, they can't help smiling back. Just try it. My son and I have had a laugh in the past by smiling at people who sometimes have to smile back even when they don't really want to. I even stopped a young guy who was walking aggressively towards me by smiling right at him. This took him completely by surprise; he smiled back and turned away from my direction. I had disarmed him with a smile! But it's a response built into human beings. Later on, I'll be sharing how clever this mechanism is at delivering a dose of feel-good hormones.

When I was on the film set, I had no idea that people thought I was upset at something, or even at them. **Unintentionally,** my facial expression affected their interaction with me. Do you know what I had to practise doing for the rest of the 10-week film shoot? Putting a big grin on whenever I was in public. Oh my, it was hard work; my face ached for days because smiling wasn't its *natural countenance*. But it worked and I ended up getting along with everyone just fine after that.

Q What does your face look like when it's at rest?

Your face is a powerful communication tool and it can change relationships. Have a look at yourself right now, and then tell yourself you look good. You might as well while you're there!

The power of a smile

When we moved into our first new house in Longton, it was clear that one of the neighbours wasn't happy. The road was a little cul-de-sac of 20 retirement bungalows, very quiet and peaceful. A builder approached 2 of the home owners with an offer to pay them thousands of pounds to buy the land in between their properties. This land was needed in order to create an access to the field behind where they were going to build some more houses. The 2 owners, I'll call them A and M, made a pact to stick together and refuse the builder's offer. Without their consent, the builder could do nothing because this was the only available access.

Subsequently, M found out that the builder had bought A's bungalow and would use its front garden to gain access. They moved out overnight with an extra cash gift in consideration of the valuable access they had now obtained. M was furious and over the next few months, he became a pain in the backside as the sales negotiator tried to sell the new estate. He would welcome every visitor with negative comments, 'You know that's a flood field don't you? Your property will be flooded.' Or he would just stand outside scowling as people viewed the houses. *He reflected how all the other elderly neighbours felt.*

We were the first people to move into one of the new houses and, on the day we did so, I had the feeling that we weren't wanted. It wasn't our fault; we were only buying what had been built but there was a ray of hope on our first night when a lovely old gentleman called Jack, came from one of the bungalows to wish us well in our new home. That made me feel better and I made sure that every time someone moved into one of the new houses, I would knock on their door with a card to pass on his welcome in return.

However, as the months went on, there was a clear division between the old and new residents. As you drove past the bungalows, if any folks were in the street, they seemed to turn away to show their feelings. Being a Christian, I talked with my husband Tony about what we could do to change the atmosphere, not just for our benefit but for theirs as well. We decided that if we caught sight of M, we would give him the sweetest smile ever and, after a few weeks, the smile was returned. (Probably the mirror neuron factor!) Over time, the smile turned into a smile and a nod, and then a wave was added. The occasional thumbs up from our then 2-year-old son James, was copied back. This went on for almost a year.

One day, as I was driving past, M motioned me to stop. I wound down the window excited to hear what he was going to say. I knew it would be positive. 'Do you know?' he said. 'You're the only ones that ever smile at me out of all that new lot. They're all so miserable.' I stayed chatting with him for about 5 minutes and as soon as I arrived home, I rang Tony to tell him what an impact our smiling had made.

You see, when you smile at someone, it could be that you are the only person who has been pleasant and friendly towards them that day, or indeed ever, as was the case with our dear neighbour who sadly died 13 weeks later unexpectedly. But our short friendship made it possible to comfort and support his sister who lived with him.

A smile brings acceptance and it's free to use

That day, I learned the power of a smile and, before 2 years was up I had made friends with all but 3 out of the 18 bungalows on my street. Old and new residents became a community and many in the new houses were able to enjoy the more relaxed atmosphere at last.

I have just begun a new technique of smiling when my teenage son starts getting on my nerves. I know that I'm controlling my reaction to him instead of shouting and screaming as I have done. It's made me feel a whole lot better especially as I've noticed he's annoyed at the fact that I'm smiling! Tee Hee. But shh, don't tell!

Social Confidence

Building a better rapport with people

No matter how confident we appear, we can sometimes struggle when we meet new people. I know I did until I read up on how to overcome these awkward situations. It's not just new people; it can be folks you know that you don't really connect with.

 I remember on one occasion collecting my son from a play date and, instead of coming down from the lad's bedroom right away, he ignored my request several times. Eventually, I ran out of things to say to the boy's mother. We just stood there speechless both getting very embarrassed and uncomfortable at not having anything to say to each other. Boy, did James get a scolding on the way home!

I decided I would never let myself get into that kind of situation again. If you attend this part of the course, it's at this point that I give out a sheet of questions called 'Who has'. Basically, there are about 27 boxes with all kinds of questions in each one. From, 'Who sleeps in the nude?' to 'Who prefers coffee to tea?' The idea is to go and ask the questions to each person in turn and find one person in the group to sign their name in that box. The first person to fill all the boxes wins a prize. Sometimes, I can hardly get the ladies to stop their noisy chattering as they determinedly go round getting the boxes filled! If I had just set the task of finding out one thing about each person, it would be a very different game.

You see **it's the prepared questions that are the key to social confidence.**

My husband confirmed this when I told him about my research. He said that whenever he goes on a sales call, he will sit and chat to the receptionist asking all manner of questions he knows off by heart. Then when he meets the person he is due to see, he always has something to talk about as he recalls various bits of information gleaned in the waiting area. For Tony, he does this so often that it is <u>natural and not forced</u>. It has become second nature so it doesn't feel like hard work.

Remember when you were learning to drive how complicated everything was, trying to coordinate all those bits of information? But, within a few weeks, you don't even think about performing different tasks with your foot, arm and eyes simultaneously. And so it is with asking questions in a social situation. The following are prepared questions to a certain degree and I'm going to give you an easy to remember mnemonic to enable you to think on your feet. As you ask the question, look for any similarities to allow you both to connect quickly. There's nothing better than discovering you went to the same school, come from the same village etc.

F.O.R.E.D

Technique

Let the person's Forehead (play on words) remind you of this technique. It helps as you will be staring at it anyway.

F is for Family. Are you married? Any children? Live in the area? The answers can lead to further questions e.g. How long have you been married? How old are your children? Etc.

O is for Occupation. Do you work? What do you do? How long have you done that? Most people are doing something. Even if they are retired, they have a work history.

R is for Recreation. What do you like doing in your spare time? What's your best achievement? How did you get into that?

E is for Education. Good one for youngsters especially. What are you doing at school, college, university? Do you know what career you want in the future?

D is for Dreams. What do you hope to do in the future? Have you got a bucket list?

These techniques do work but I have sometimes found myself unable to ask any of the above questions because they weren't appropriate. It's at that point when 'Do you come here often?' isn't as cheesy as it would be in a dating situation. It can often break the ice as you both laugh away.

My dad often opens our conversations with a sentence he's comfortable with; it makes me laugh because he says it automatically as soon he sees me. 'What do you know this week that you didn't know last?' I just laugh because I have to think for a minute. But you could think of your own line that will become second nature. Here's mine, which I think is a pearl. *'What have you been up to this week?'* It allows them to spill their news until you can pick up on something they say. If they say 'nothing much' you can then launch into what you have been doing. Well, they had their chance didn't they?!

Going Blank

It's embarrassing when you have just been introduced to someone and, within a few seconds, you've forgotten their name. Yes, I know you are nodding in agreement and, unfortunately, it gets worse with age! So here are a few things to help.

As you meet them, shake their hand (if it's offered) and *say* 'Pleased to meet you Mary' (or whatever their name is!). This reinforces it in your memory because you have said it out loud.

Another is to *repeat* the name in your head furiously *five* times. If you can say it differently each time it tends to stick. (Pronounce it differently e.g. Mare re)

Another is to try to *liken that person to a friend* you already have. Same colour of hair, got a beard or glasses etc. Not always easy to do but sometimes it will fit the bill quite readily.

58

Do you know why it is that we forget someone's name upon first meeting them?

It's because *we are not listening;* we are often *worrying about what we are going to say next*! So if you apply the **FORED** technique, it should help.

Here are 2 gems that I've used very successfully when someone has been looming towards me and I should know their name but have forgotten it.

'Oh no' you think; this is going to be embarrassing!

 If you have someone with you and they already know them, you can just smile in the hope that the name will slip out. That's been a lifesaver for me. However, if the person you are with doesn't know them, you can take the initiative and as the nameless person approaches you can say, 'Hi, this is George.'(Pointing to your friend). 'Would you like to introduce yourself?' This is really good, but the next one is a gem.

You are on your own and they loom ever nearer. Say 'Hi' then immediately say 'What's your name again?' Now they will give you their first name. To which you reply laughing, 'No, not your first name, your surname.' Ha-ha, you've got it - now try to learn it! (We can all be forgiven for forgetting a surname!)

I've employed all the above techniques very *successfully* so get practising them and *grow* in social confidence. Then you can move on to something that's more challenging.

How to break the ice in a lift!

Why, oh why, do most folk stop talking when they enter a lift?

I often get the giggles at the silence and want to say something like, 'Shall we say weeeeeee as we descend?' Or I repeat every floor number as if I'm the official lift operator. Once, as I got into the lift on a cruise ship, I said, 'Let's all stand this way eh' and refused to turn towards the door as is the usual custom. Everyone was laughing at the end as I walked out backwards, not to be defeated. It's even funnier if you have your back to the doors when they open. You can have a lot of fun with a chum in a lift, but you are viewed as somewhat strange if you are on your own and don't conform to the lift rules. It's a funny old world.

Try not to forget that often the other person is just as nervous as you, so relax.

A guaranteed way to quickly make friends

 I was 16 before I ever went out for a meal with friends. Yes, I lived a sheltered life. It was the works' 'Christmas do' and the waitress was coming round with coffee asking everyone whether they wanted black or white. I was confused because not being a big caffeine fan, I was unsure which I preferred. So I asked, 'Have you any *brown* coffee?' Everyone roared with laughter at my ignorance and so did I eventually. Thing is, this is a funny little story that I have ready to drop into my conversations.

Skilled communicators always have many incidents and experiences that they can draw on. The results often produce laughter, which is a unique trait of human beings. Laughter develops a connectedness that catapults you into a safe zone in the person's mind, quickly building your relationship, particularly if it's something you have experienced together. More on the power of laughter later on.

 **Q** What funny stories do you have? The more embarrassing, the better. Well you've got to laugh at yourself sometimes haven't you?

Don't forget to smile at every opportunity.

Proverbs 15v30. A cheerful look brings joy to the heart. (NIV 1984 edition)

- We're worth it.

- Write down your attributes and shout them out.

- Your words bring life and death.

- Learn to like and love yourself.

- Building up others also builds *your* self - esteem.

- Add value to others.

- Thank the people in your life.

- Smile more often!

- Prepared questions are the key.

- Use F.O.R.E.D

- Listen to their name.

- Have a funny story to tell.

1

Some paraphrased verses to build you up - say them out loud!

I am chosen.	John 15:16
You sing over me with pleasure.	Zephaniah 3:17
I can approach God's throne in confidence.	Hebrews 4:16
You loved me first.	1 John 4:19
You count my steps.	Job 31:4
You will not leave me.	Hebrews 13:5
I am part of your family.	1 Timothy 3:15
You paid a great price for me.	1 Corinthians 6:20
I belong to you.	Romans 7:14
Every day of my life is recorded.	Psalm 139:16
I am His child.	Galatians 3:26
His eye is upon me.	Psalm 33:18
He loved me first.	1 John 4:19
I am the apple of God's eye.	Psalm 17:8
I am held in the palm of His hand.	Isaiah 49:16
He takes pleasure in me.	Psalm 147:11
I belong to Him.	Romans 7:4
He will take care of me.	Isaiah 46:4

You carefully designed me.   Psalm 139:13-14

You have set me apart for special work.   Jeremiah 1:5

He has good thoughts about me.   Jeremiah 29:11

You can have faith because:

All things work together for those who love God.   Romans 8:28

I can do all things through Christ.   Philippians 4:13

No weapon fashioned against me shall prosper.   Isaiah 54:17

I have been chosen and appointed to bear fruit.   John 15:16

I can cast all my cares on Him.   1 Peter 5:7

Your word is my guiding light.   Psalm 119:105

I am not fearful but bold, loving and sensible.   2 Timothy 1:7

You are secure in Him

I am able to rest under God's mighty protection.   Psalm 91:1

I have been bought at a price. I belong to God.   1 Corinthians 6:19-20

I cannot be separated from the love of God.   Romans 8:35

I am a citizen of heaven.   Philippians 3:20

I am free from condemnation.   Romans 8:1-2

I am etched on the palm of His hand.   Isaiah 49:16

I stand firm in Christ who guarantees what is to come.
     2 Corinthians 1:21-22

What's my Purpose?

Confidence to go for it

As I studied to produce my Confidence Gym course, I came across some information from nurses. They noticed that elderly people would often voice their regrets for not having done all manner of things in their younger years when they were fit and healthy. The knowledge that it was now too late made them feel frustrated and sad which in turn, took its toll on their health. (More about that in Session 3).

On her 90th birthday, I asked my great-aunt Amy if she could still remember her youth. I was surprised when she said it felt like yesterday and in her words, "Life is so short Susan." When you quantify the average life expectancy in weeks, it's very thought provoking. Seventy-five years equates to 3,900 weeks which makes me shudder as I'm already at 2,840! My aunt lived for 4,965 weeks which is significantly above average but she had no way of knowing just how long she would survive. I think she lived to a ripe old age because she was active and occupied. She did voluntary work well into her 80s and even got married again at 75! It's interesting that when God created Adam, He put him in the garden to work, not to sit and chill!

You have to make the most of every week you have.

Psalm90v12 So teach us to number our days, that we may apply our hearts to wisdom. (NKJV)

Q Tot up the number of weeks you've already lived.

In this first section, I want to give you the desire to discover what it is you are here for and to help you understand that there's everything to play for if you really want it.

Why is it important to have a feeling of purpose and fulfil it?

This next exercise was a turning point in my life. I'm not being morbid but it does help to focus your thoughts on *what you have been doing so far.*

Q If you were to die tomorrow, what would the epitaph on your tombstone say?

It was only when I looked at this in an *objective way* that I could truly identify what my *heart's desire* really was. Up to this point, the only thing I could have put on the headstone was, 'She liked dancing!' I wanted to be remembered for something more than that!

I was so disappointed. Yes, it would also say mother to James and beloved wife of Tony and creating a loving home was always my top priority but I wanted more, and I could give more. I felt it was the route to being fully alive and kicking.

As I *put some more thought* into what I wanted it to read, I found my mind focussing on ways I could achieve it. I wanted my epitaph to read, '*She made a difference.*' The creative possibilities are endless as I'm good at creative things (but rubbish at maths) but the main thing that let me down was that I never strive for excellence. I always want a quick fix so that gives me an *it will do* mind-set, wanting to accomplish lots of things instead of one great thing. Knowing your faults can be very helpful so ask someone you trust to be honest with you.

Proverbs20v18 Form your purpose by asking for council (The Message)

Q How could I improve in this area?

When I asked my husband Tony he said, 'You'll only make a difference when you stick to one thing! Focus on one thing and don't get distracted.' I was into all sorts but without me realising, they were all contributing towards my one big thing.

Firstly, I want to tell you where I was career-wise so that you can see the journey I made. I had a good career in advertising, training and printing in that order. I then left work completely to bring up my longed for son James. When he was 8, I began to work part-time in my husband's business and do volunteer work in the village community through my church. Despite all this busyness, *I felt lost* and unable to grasp the new computer technology that had taken over the workplace. I tried my hand at different skills but over time, if you are not keeping yourself up to date, you will actually fall behind. Nothing stands still! I remember attending a training session where we told about the *Kaizen* business strategy, which is a Japanese word meaning *Continuous Improvement*. What really hit home for me was when we were told, 'Others will surpass you if you don't progress.' A case in point is The Swiss Clocks Company Ltd, an established and highly profitable business, which was swamped in the digital era; they hadn't thought that watch making would ever need to change.

Don't get too comfy

At any time, we can be hit with thoughts that we've gone as far as we're able. From the age of 52 I've had middle-aged thinking; willing to settle for less and getting comfy in that armchair each evening. *Contentment can be your enemy.*

When I was 45, a friend told me about a couple at her church that had just given up serving because they were in their 50s and felt they'd *done enough* and wanted a rest. She said they still had a lot to offer and she couldn't understand why they seemed to be giving up on life at such a relatively young age. At the time I didn't give it any further thought but when I reached 50 I began to understand what she was getting at. I resolved that I wouldn't give up but start to believe that my best years were ahead!

Research shows that we all have an area of excellence - abilities that exceed others. The Bible confirms that God has a special unique assignment for each of us, something that only we are commissioned to do: something of value to the human race. That's so exciting!

We are God's handiwork, created in Christ Jesus to do good works, which God prepared for us in advance to do.

(Ephesians 2:10 NIV)

My mum-in-law Betty used to love watching a TV programme about dilapidated houses bought at auction. The buyers were asked what they were planning to do and it was interesting to catch up with them 6 months later to see the results. I wouldn't even attempt to transform a dilapidated old house but there are people out there who do because *they have the ability to see its potential*. They often have problems to solve but in the end it's very profitable and creates a desirable place to live. This idea can be transferred into our thinking. If we just put some time and effort into our lives, the results are always amazing. I hope that's why you're reading this book because you want to live the best life you can and become the best possible version of you.

Don't underestimate your value and significance

Like the property buyers, it's other people that can see the possibilities in you. Every human being is born with promise but so often, we fail to use our imagination, inventiveness and unique genius. Our originality is linked to our self-worth but as children, we are told to colour within the lines. This does have its value in teaching discipline but it also imposes restraint and discourages imaginative thinking which goes outside boundaries. We learn that it's not smart to stand out so we go along with the crowd, never allowing our natural gifts to appear. Discouragement has a lot to answer for *but* creativity and talent can be unearthed at any time.

As we grow older and more secure, we can discover it all again

When I was 30 my life was in disarray. I cried on my birthday because I hadn't managed to conceive. I was stressed with the medical treatments and interventions and it hurt every time I heard a friend announce that she was pregnant. I felt such a failure. Time passed and I got my beloved baby boy but I wasn't really doing anything with myself. I was on auto drive, cruising along in life, taking part in this or that but never *feeling accomplished* at anything.

Then I was forced to read a book. I wasn't a big reader and apart from the Bible, the last thing I'd read was Enid Blyton! In 1999, one of our church leaders bought 50 copies - one for each family - of a book he felt would *transform* us all. I was cross that he'd wasted church funds on books which I thought were a complete waste of time. I wasn't interested in reading anything and I particularly disliked being told that I had to. *I assumed that others felt like me.* As a church, we were to explore the book together for the next 40 days and reluctantly, I joined in. To my amazement, I was hooked from page 1 and I then realised why Mike had invested in the books for us - I couldn't put it down! The book is *The Purpose Driven Life* by Rick Warren, an American pastor. It has been massively successful, selling over 30 million copies. The book takes you on a personal 40-day spiritual journey to help you understand why you are alive and reveal God's plan for you. **It's a must-read.**

I remember it made me feel special and encouraged me to explore all my talents and gifts - I was pumped to achieve. I got into lots of different ministry areas at church eager to see where I fitted in best but where was I going to excel? Being part of a volunteer group can be very helpful at discovering what you're good at and because you're a volunteer, you can't be sacked or told off too harshly because we practice grace. In many churches, people want to become a mouthpiece when their real gift is to listen. It's like a foot trying to be a hand! Knowing how we are gifted helps us to identify where to put our focus, energy and time. The Bible tells us:

If you preach, just preach God's Message, nothing else; if you help, just help, don't take over; if you teach, stick to your teaching; if you give encouraging guidance, be careful that you don't get bossy; if you're put in charge, don't manipulate; if you're called to give aid to people in distress, keep your eyes open and be quick to respond; if you work with the disadvantaged, don't let yourself get irritated with them or depressed by them. Keep a smile on your face.

(Romans 12:6-8 The Message)

A few years later my first pastor Rob Whittaker lent me some audiotapes by Brian Tracy, an international trainer and authority on personal development. They were brilliant and still widely available – I highly recommend them. I listened to the *Psychology of Achievement*, a series of 4 audiotapes that showed you how to be a *first-class achiever* in your gifting. It's ok reading about what you need to do but if you don't know how to get there, nothing will ever change. Some of what I'm about to share in this session, is taken from what I heard.

As we learned in session 1 *we are set to negative* so in order to make it all happen; you have to set yourself a goal. This involves an investment of time.

A goal is what switches you on to success

To quote Brian Tracy, 'It's like a heat-seeking mechanism that activates the whole system – your talk, your vision, seeing things not seen before, your focus in particular, all of which enlarges your thinking.' This is so true.

We had moved into our third home. Our other houses had been brand new so we were able to put our stamp on them but this house was tired. The kitchen was big but badly laid out for cooking and eating – you couldn't even get a dining table in there. I went to bed one night wondering how I could solve this problem and then it came to me. If I took out three cupboards down the right-hand side, we'd be able to put a table there. Eureka. All of a sudden the floodgates opened and a rush of ideas came to me as I imagined how the kitchen could look and feel. The possibilities were endless and a million jobs seemed to flow into my mind - plasterer, builder, decorator and carpet fitter. I ran down to Tony who was in the middle of watching a film and burst in the door with the words, 'We're off to B&Q tomorrow!' I started explaining my solution but he couldn't catch my excitement because it hadn't been his goal; he hadn't been throwing the idea around for the last half hour. He hadn't solved the problem. So he just looked up and said, 'OK love if that's what you want' and went back to watching his film.

Don't get disappointed if people don't see what you see at first because they'll come around eventually. The next morning, he was on board saying it was a brilliant plan. Solving the problem of the table gave me such a buzz of excitement and energy; *it activated my whole system*. I hardly slept for the rest of the night with the adrenalin rush. NB – Don't set to work on a goal after 10.30pm!

Research shows that every peak performing man and woman is a goal setter

People feel at their happiest when they are thoroughly engaged in the flow of something. Here comes that 5%

statistic again - only 5% of us ever set written goals. The Bible tells us to:

Write down the vision and make it plain.

(Habakkuk 2:2 Authorised King James Version)

New Year's resolutions don't last because people never draw up *an action plan.* Every goal starts with a thought that develops into a dream. That's where it stops for many people – in their head. *Every dream needs a plan.* In the Bible, Joseph had to put an action plan together to secure Egypt's future survival. Egypt was prosperous but Joseph knew that the abundant harvests would be followed by 7 years of famine so he saved grain in anticipation of the hard times ahead. This plan saved the nation from starvation and Joseph rose to become Prime Minister.

Achieving your dreams can be hard work but *setbacks can become set-ups for you.* Plans are everything and if they are not done by you, someone else will have to do the work at some point e.g. planning a surprise party. 'Fail to plan, plan to fail' is an old saying but an accurate one. If you don't plan for the future, your future will be a failure. *Your goals and dreams will elude you.*

Proverbs21v5 *Careful planning puts you ahead in the long run. (The Message)*

A word of caution here. Desire is the root of all dreams but what price are you willing to pay? I know families that have been torn apart because the father was hell bent on promotion, chained to work and not there for his wife and children. Women in this position become emotionally and physically drained because they are parenting alone with little or no support. But I've also known women who drive their husbands into the ground with their incessant demands for more of everything that money can buy. *Is living in luxury, or becoming top dog worth the cost to your relationships?*

If your goals are big, it's going to take desire, drive and determination

They will suck you dry unless you *plan* your breathing spaces and relaxation. Learn to work around your rest times and don't let your family down by failing to take all your holiday entitlement. In your later years you won't be thinking of your bank balance but who's there to look after you and care about you. Putting family first *pays dividends.*

Some of the happiest people I know only have the basics in life. A roof, food and enough for essentials. More about this in the last session of the book.

Research shows that when goal setting is implemented, it is highly effective

You can read the various business books to confirm my findings, otherwise read on with interest.

If you can encourage children at an *early age* to set goals, it will become a *normal* part of their lives. Why are some families living on welfare benefits generation after generation? Part of the reason is that they have *never been challenged* to dig deep and discover who they are. They are not encouraged by anyone to *believe* they can achieve great things. Dreams *stay* in their heads and they live in a small world of repetition. It's always good to see lots of young people taking up new sports after the Olympics. They have seen that others can do it and something shifts inside their spirit.

If you seek you will find.

Opportunity is out there for everyone

You hear people say they're down on their luck and that good things always happen to other people, never them. There was a study conducted by Professor Richard Wiseman to see whether people would notice an opportunity right in front of their eyes. The participants were asked to count the pictures in a broadsheet newspaper but over half of them failed to see a half-page advert offering a £250 prize if they

75

spotted it. When we are narrow minded, we don't see what is around us just waiting to be grabbed. At another of my sessions I repeat this experiment with 2 or 3 posters dotted around the place saying if you spot this Susan will give you a sweet. Each time it's only between 1 and 2% that notices it. There are always people who say they saw it but didn't know what it was, were too afraid to collect the sweet or didn't want to draw attention to themselves.

 **Q** What is going on under your nose that you might be missing? Face book groups you could join, learning or inspirational podcasts you could be listening to. My son James always fails to find chocolate hidden in the kitchen because he only ever looks in the same cupboards.

It's not the luckiest people that get the most out of life but *those who look more*. So let's start to dig down deeper.

What is a goal?

Whether it's big or small, achieving your goal builds self-esteem and increases that *can-do attitude*. Confidence is built as a small foundation and setting some additional small goals can add some walls and floors. *Remember, step by step.*

How do you know it's the right goal?

 At this point it's worth taking time to answer a few questions about yourself and your situation.

Q1. Are you happy as you are?

Q2. If time and money were not an issue what would you try to do? Why would you want to do this? What is your motive?

Q3. Can you think of 3 goals right now big or small?

Q4. What would you do if you won £1,000, £100,000, £500,000 or even a million or 2? You will discover that you reach a point where the numbers don't really matter because you have enough to make your dreams a reality. Most of you have probably dreamt of winning a million already so get those creative juices flowing and see what you come up with. You might find a deep-seated urge to start a hospital in Zambia or a halfway house for folks beat up with life. Really worthwhile projects that mean you become fully alive and not just exist. Or you might just be content to pay off your mortgage and treat the grandchildren and that's fine too because we are all uniquely different.

Q5. If you learned you were going to die in 6 months time, what would your priorities be?

Q6. What has been your greatest achievement in life so far? Or made you the happiest? Or given you the greatest feeling of importance? How did it make you feel? What difference has it made to your life?

Stick with the thought process; you are chewing the cud, like a cow, *getting the most out of this.*

All the answers to these questions are designed to reveal your priorities in life. What has come out on top? Self-achievement; caring for others; life experiences; the desire to do your best; a willingness to work hard for what you get?

Your priorities are yours alone so don't compete or compare with anyone else.

Taking this time to think about what you want out of life is *paramount* to the goal setting you will do.

Some of you will have skipped the questions. Is that the way you do life?

Before a caterpillar emerges into that beautiful butterfly, it retreats for months into a cocoon-like structure called a chrysalis. If you were to split open the chrysalis in the early stage you would just find a DNA soup of mixed up juices because the caterpillar almost liquefies in order to achieve its transformation.

So although the questions are taxing and may even cause a little discomfort and confusion, it is worth it in the end. People are often unwilling to tackle questions that reveal motives they may be ashamed of or embarrassed about. It can also be difficult discovering likes, dislikes and character traits. A bit of a mess like the DNA soup but aren't *you worth it*?

If it's easier, ask a friend these questions and do it as a talking point. Make it a relaxing exercise.

Goals wake you up and excite you

You will know it's the right goal because it grips you with a passion. It won't leave you alone and you can't escape from it. *You start to see opportunities for it to flourish and your brain marks out things you hadn't noticed before.*

Our aim should be to find out what it is that we are passionate about. Research shows that you can only do something really well when you are passionate about it. That's why for Olympians, it's not a drudge going to the pool at 5am everyday and spending 12 hours practising.

Many people spend 15-20 years in dead-end jobs. They provide an income but, without passion, there is *no job satisfaction, joy or fulfilment*. This does nothing for your self-esteem.

 Write down all the things you love doing. Look at your diary. What have you already been involved in; what were you excited by; what hobbies do you have? Go to a magazine shop and browse the shelves. You'll be amazed at the number of different hobby and interest magazines there are now.

After I had read *The Purpose Driven Life*, I asked my husband Tony what he thought I was good at and straight away, he said it was sharing information. He didn't mean that I'm a gossip but if I find out something new that can benefit others; I want to tell as many people as possible. *Wow, a light went on as I realised he was right.* Sometimes other people that love you and want the best for you are better at showing you or identifying your talent and gifting.

That Christmas I'd visited my niece who showed me one of her Christmas presents, a book called *A Box of Delights* by J John and Mark Stibbe. It's a collection of heart-warming tales and quotations and it really caught my attention because I'd never seen anything quite like it before. As I whizzed through the pages, I was filled with joy. It had such an effect on me that I went to the bookshop and bought it along with every other title in the series and read them all from cover to cover. What Tony had said about me wanting to share new information with people was so true because I'd bought 10 more copies and given them out as late Christmas presents. *I wanted to share the positive experience* with others to make them smile. I was gripped with a passion to promote these books and their uplifting qualities so I told everybody I met about them and bought more copies to give as birthday presents, thank you gifts and such like. (They are still available and the titles are shown in the index).

When you become aware of what it is that excites you, you will subconsciously focus on it

When you're on a cruise there's lots of on-board entertainment and activities for you to choose from and that's how I came to attend a series of talks by Diane Simpson, a graphologist who had worked with the police. She analyses the physical characteristics and patterns of handwriting to identify the writer and evaluate their psychological state and personality characteristics. As you all know by now, I love science so I really enjoyed learning about her *Mind Games* as she called them.

After hearing Diane, it suddenly occurred to me that I too could talk to people about a subject I was interested in. At school I always relished the opportunity to do a talk to my English class. My first one was about keeping a tortoise and much to everyone's amusement, especially my teachers, I even explained how they had sex. I'd had 2 tortoises as a youngster so I'd seen it happen often enough and I wasn't in the least embarrassed to explain it and demonstrate it too! I loved my tortoise Jack so much that when he died, I had him scraped out by a taxidermist and kept his shell, which I used for the sex demonstration to show how the underside is concave so that the male can mount the female. I always remember making everyone laugh. This was a significant confidence builder at the time.

My second talk at school was about ants (perhaps not quite as interesting as tortoises) and I also ran a nature club for the kids in my street because I wanted to tell them all about wildlife, trees and plants. This desire to inform people *was in my blood all the time.*

It just took something to *ignite* it so that my subconscious would reach into my inner desire.

It may be worth taking note of your Childs interests when they are young, to relay them when they come to a time of making important decisions.

Albert Einstein, the German physicist said,' Your imagination is your preview of life's coming attractions.' One of the things you can do to focus on your dreams is play them out as a mini film in your mind. See it at its highest and greatest – really feel the exuberance. I actually did this when I was 24. You'll remember from the beginning of the book that Tony came home and told me he wanted a divorce. 'Forget him,' I said to myself, 'I'm going to write a book and become really famous.' As a teenager, I loved writing up my diary every night with pages and pages about the day's events and experiences. Until the age of 14, I was an avid Enid Blyton fan and my head was always full of new adventures to be shared with the world. I imagined that my book would be published and I'd receive a top literary award as well.

I could visualise myself collecting the award to the tune of *Wishful Thinking* by China Crisis and I could hear the thunderous applause from the admiring audience. Even now, 30 years later, I can still remember those feelings of pride, joy and achievement. Because of all the research I've done, I know that these memories and feelings are still strong because I created an **emotion** that was set into my mind.

These emotions are real and they can drive you on towards achieving your goal

Your mind starts to notice anything connected to your goal because when you focus on it you will see things you *previously missed.*

When I started my career in advertising sales, I worked in an office dominated by men. One of them was very attractive, a bit like Orlando Bloom in his early twenties, and I became a bit besotted with everything he did and liked. His journey to work took him near my house so he offered to give me a lift every morning in his red Ford Escort. I'd never had any particular interest in cars (and still don't!) but suddenly, I was very interested in Ford Escorts and started to see them everywhere. It seemed as if every other car was one but the reality was that the circumstances had made me aware of something that I hadn't noticed before. I was dating my husband to be at this point and he decided to get a yellow Ford Escort probably to compete for my affections. The gorgeous salesman left the company 4 months later and Tony has always checked up on how the guy has faired over the years, proudly showing me a picture 10 years ago of a balding guy with a beer belly saying look at him now Susan. My husband is still gorgeous and has all his hair too!

Research says that whatever you hold in your mind i.e. focus on and visualise, you can accomplish

When I realised that I wanted to help others achieve their full potential, I would imagine myself speaking to large groups of ladies, as I would go about my daily routines, particularly in bathroom mode between toothpaste and face cream.

 One day, a friend asked me if I could do a 10-minute talk at a ladies' strawberries and cream afternoon tea. When she said the topic was *The Differences Between Men and Women,* I was so excited because I'd just finished reading a book on that very subject. I eagerly agreed and my speaking notes and the jokes I'd been rehearsing, flowed effortlessly onto the paper. *I imagined it going very well with everyone laughing* and guess what, they did. I'd successfully completed my first public speaking event and it had just been offered to me on a plate!

I now knew I had the skills set to deliver science and laughter in an interesting way and I was particularly drawn to researching confidence building. I didn't know how it would all pan out as a 6-session course but I visualised it and entrusted it to God.

 *Using visualisation is a mental marathon* that you run in your mind every day. Sports people do this regularly, not just training their bodies but their minds as well, seeing themselves winning.

When we focus on something we magnify it and that's why it shouldn't be a negative

A while ago there was a brilliant programme on Channel 4 called *Faking It* which demonstrated the power of focus and mental programming. It featured people who were dissatisfied with their jobs or had a desire to try something different and gave them the opportunity to receive intense training and mentoring with an expert for 4 weeks. For example, there was a burger van proprietor who trained with Gordon Ramsay to become a cordon bleu chef; a classical violinist who wanted to become a rap DJ; a lap dancer who wanted to be a ballet dancer and a priest who wondered what it would be like to be a second-hand car salesman. At the end of 4 weeks, the test was to see whether they could fake it in front of a panel of judges who were the leading experts in that particular field. And the answer was yes, most of the time they did it! They were *passionate* about what they wanted and what was particularly striking was that they started behaving and dressing as top performers in their chosen profession. This was a *key moment* in each show because it spurred them on even more and gave them the passion and focus to make amazing career and life changes. They had the right help but they still had to put in all the hard work. They did have low points but after some *encouragement and tough love*, they reapplied themselves and soldiered on.

Have a think about *your* hobbies and interests and what you could achieve with them. For instance, if you love baking, why not supply local shops with your goodies? Could you turn your gardening passion into a business? A knitter or artist selling on the web? The exciting possibilities are endless! You'll all have heard of the businessman and celebrity chef, Levi Roots. For years, he made his now famous Reggae Reggae Sauce in his Brixton kitchen with the help of his children. He would go out on the streets and sell it out of a backpack. In 2006 he sold 4000 bottles at the Notting Hill Carnival which spurred him on to take it to a trade show and then to appear on *Dragons' Den.* Despite being told by one of the dragons that there was no future in his business idea, he went on to build a brand which is now worth over £30 million. In his words, 'If a black Brixtonian Rastafarian can make it with just a sauce, then you can make it too.'

 Why not jot down some of the things you like doing? Test drive your ideas to see what people think of them.

You will have talents and gifts that excel all others

You do need to stay in your gifting though and if you're really passionate about something, there's a good chance it will be a great success. After all, we go to see people who are at the top of their game, not the *X Factor* hopefuls who think they can sing. I love singing but I'm only a 4 out of 10 talent wise so no one would enjoy a night listening to me. My real passion was dancing but my raw talent made me 7 out of 10 at best. Just think, if I could go back in time and get the sort of training and encouragement given to the *Faking It* contestants, I could be judging *Strictly Come Dancing* now! I have used this gift of dance to great effect in the church over the years and I loved all the dance workshops and dramas I performed with my company Calvary Dance, as we shared the love of Jesus up and down the country. None of us were professionally trained but the Holy Spirit gave us wonderful ideas and many goose bump moments that I still carry with me today. I had a blast. I'll reveal something special I learned about dancing in the last session.

 Listen to this little *gem* of a story I heard as I began to compile my data for this session. There was an old African farmer who had done well in life but his land had never yielded a massive profit. He was excited when he heard about the pioneers who were discovering diamond mines further south so he sold his land and went off to try and find a mine to buy. After an exhaustive search and many years wandering the vast continent of Africa, he committed suicide on a beach. Many years later the man who had bought his farm was out walking with a friend and picked up a stone that threw off light in an unusual manner. His friend recognised it as a rough diamond and it turned out that the whole farm was covered in acres of diamonds. All the time the African farmer had everything he was looking for right under his nose but *he didn't know what to look for.*

Opportunities come as rough diamonds that can be made to shine when we put some work in

It's all usually close at hand so look right where you are.

When I heard this, I realised that *everything* I had done up to that point was like those *rough diamonds.*

My children's acting club had built my confidence because I had to perform with the children and organise events for parents to attend. Brownie guiding taught me that people learn more quickly when they are playing a game. All my sales and advertising experience enabled me to market myself to the right people. Unknowingly, I had tested out all my material with a Ladies' Life Group at church. I had passionately researched the idea of confidence building and was convinced it was a skill that could be taught. The next step was to *polish all my findings and get them to sparkle and shine.*

My research took 4 years (and it's still ongoing) and I was always on the lookout for the latest information and scientific findings. The only problem was how to get speaking engagements but then, I got an unexpected break. My friend Carol Halton, who was also interested in the subject of confidence building, was due to speak at a conference in Blackpool and asked me to go along to support her. I was keen to learn all I could from any experience but 2 days before the conference she suggested that I should deliver some of the material I'd been telling her about and do half the seminar with her. It was a frightening prospect but I saw this as a God-given opportunity and grabbed it with both hands. That day will be forever etched on my mind. The feedback was so encouraging and the ladies loved my games and thought-provoking challenges.

Carol then suggested doing a full seminar at her house one evening. When 17 ladies said they were eager to come, we knew we'd hit on something that they were struggling with. That night was great fun and the response afterwards confirmed that everything I had imagined and visualised was becoming a reality. I knew I'd found my purpose – this is what I'm on the planet to do!

Carol then got going with organising conference rooms in hotels and women were pushing me to come up with more and more topics. The material just flowed supernaturally from all my previous learning - books, TV programmes and tapes just coming into my world at the right moment. I'll never forget it. So **Confidence Gym – a Workout for Your Self-Esteem** was born. Before I knew it, I was travelling up and down the country visiting all kinds of organisations that had groups of women eager to be empowered.

Goal setting brings positivity into your life and mind

Another reason to have a goal is that it can enable you to control the direction of change. Your life can be like a car on the road without a driver at the wheel. You're prone to crashes and scrapes sometimes ending up in a ditch where you need help to get back on the road.

A goal is like always holding the wheel, giving you the power to steer yourself in the right direction.

Barriers to fulfilling your destiny

Hopefully, you are now ready to go and set some goals. Later, I'll be giving you the expertise to do it but first of all, let's tackle the reasons why many people fail to make their dreams a reality.

1.   Fear of what people think

Being judged too adventurous

It's annoying when people say, 'Oh I wouldn't do that if I were you!' but that's what I said to Tony when he announced that he was going to start an advertising agency at the start of a recession! Fortunately, he ignored me and built a successful company which is still going strong after 25 years.

Such opinions can fill you with self doubt and make you feel that what you've set out to do is way beyond your capabilities but actually, what the person has said is that *it's beyond their capabilities!* They think that because *they couldn't do it, no one else can* but that's because they have a fearful and narrow mindset. Take a balanced view of people's comments and don't let them *put you off before you've even got going!*

Jealousy can sometimes rear its ugly head

You may be eager to share your dreams but not everyone is going to be interested and happy for you. This is because your plans can make them *feel* inadequate but that's not your fault, it's their problem. Don't dwell on it, just walk around them mentally. I've found that the best course of action is to only share my ideas with like-minded people because *they will see what others don't.* They'll be your cheerleaders and encourage you every step of the way.

I was blessed to have Carol Halton in my life and God certainly knew what he was doing when our friendship started back in 1986. But it was 20 years later before our work together began. Take a look around you and you will see that there are people in your life that could play a

87

part in your plan; *they will step onto your stage right on cue. Your relationships are one of your best resources.*

As a child, you never had fears about what you wanted to be, you just saw it modelled somewhere in your world or on TV and wanted to go for it. Remember those words, 'When I grow up I'm going to be a .... '

 As far back as I can remember, my childhood dream was to be a naturalist like David Attenborough though embarrassingly, I often used to say naturist until I learned the difference! I even used to talk to an imaginary TV video camera describing all the trees and flowers in the local woods. But despite getting good marks in science subjects and having the ability to do presentations in English lessons, I never pursued my dreams; boys *distracted* me and my marks slipped. Career opportunities were not the same when I was a girl so after only a 5-minute chat, The Careers Office offered me retail or factory work so my dream of being a naturalist was forgotten. But guess what - with the advent of Face book and blogging, I now post on nature as part of my newsfeed. People say they love it so in a small way, I've realised my childhood dream. I'm convinced that destiny reveals itself to us and is in us, right from the start so just because you missed your chance years ago, doesn't mean it's too late. Two of my cousins missed out on going to university at 18 but finally achieved it in their 30s.

One of the exercises I do in this session at Confidence Gym is to get everyone to say what their childhood dream was. They can all remember it but only 5-10% ever went on to achieve it often because of distraction or self doubt. I hope you'll be encouraged by my husband Tony's story.

 As a youngster, he enjoyed making movies with his father, the old 8mm reels. It then got forgotten about and as a teenager, his family persuaded him to get a trade as was the custom back then. He ended up training as a motor mechanic with disastrous consequences

(crashing one car and reversing into a bollard to mention a couple). Leaving school with 1 O Level didn't qualify him to go to film school but through a series of God opportunities, Tony discovered at the age of 45 that he was still interested in film and began to teach himself off the web. The new digital era made filmmaking accessible to everyone so he jumped right in.

On a church trip to London to learn more about worship (Tony played guitar), he saw that they presented their notices in a TV style advert. It seemed current and interesting and he remembered all the news items in detail. He saw an opportunity to copy this at our church and approached the Elders with the idea. Our niece had taken a media degree so together they produced *Church News* in 2006. He loved learning this new medium because it was in his DNA and it didn't feel like work because he was so passionate about it. He would spend 5 hours every night learning his new craft and then all kinds of short films began to appear in his portfolio. If you have been to Confidence Gym you may have seen the *Top Ten Tips* DVD. This was his first little film and it's brought so much laughter over the years. (Check out my website at suainsworth.co.uk as I may have permission to show it there). When he sees this DVD now, he cringes at its technical structure because he has *continued to learn and develop* his skills.

What happened next is amazing. Someone from Tony's advertising agency saw *Church News* and suggested that he should do a film to promote the company. He wasn't particularly proud of it but nonetheless, a client saw it and thought that Tony's ideas were perfect for their business and ordered a film. That was back in 2009 and the film work increased to such a degree that making corporate films became a significant part of the business. He put so much work into polishing this *rough diamond* that in 2015 he saw his first TV programme broadcast on BBC4 *Inside Sellafield* and at the moment has 2 other documentaries in the pipeline which will air in 2016. Tony has been able to realise his boyhood dream because he *saw an opportunity and acted upon it*.

Think carefully about the things you feel passionate about and don't give up on them.

2. Fear of change

This fear is usually in our subconscious. We have a natural tendency to stay in our comfort zone because we feel safe when we are dealing with the familiar. *But once you make a change, it quickly becomes the norm.* Although I've already covered this in the first session, here are some more thoughts connected to purpose that I'd like to add.

Keep on doing what you keep on doing and you'll keep on getting what you keep on getting.

When you're stuck in a rut it stops you from opening your eyes to see all the possibilities. I used to be terrible at making a change and I would only do so when it was forced upon me. I've now learned to recognise that this is my default setting and not let it slow me down. It's a kind of laziness I suppose.

Having a *positive attitude* towards change is the key to growth. My milkman kept getting my order wrong because he didn't read the notes that I left out for him. I ended up with either too much milk, which was thrown away, or none at all! Reluctantly, I started buying milk from the supermarket when I ran short and found that it was much more efficient. That relatively small change was forced upon me and it had a good outcome but when it's something really important it can be really scary if you don't apply positive thinking.

In April 1989 when my husband sprang it on me that he was going to give up his job and start his own advertising business, I began to get very worried. My wage wouldn't be enough and how would we manage without the company car? He was completely confident that all would be well but *I could only focus on the negatives.* Fortunately, just as Tony resigned I changed my job for one with a company car. My new job was also a change of career so I had to travel to London for a month's training. My work area was the whole of northwest England and as I hated driving, the anxiety gave me a stress rash for 6 months! BUT I DID IT SCARED!

I prayed for that job to end because I was so miserable. However, my good work ethic got me noticed in the company and I began to shine as one of the top merchandisers. This built my confidence enormously and I believed I now had the skills, *albeit forced on me,* to get another job where I didn't have to work 7 days a week and do so much driving. When the company decided to downsize because of the recession, they wanted me to stay on but relocate to another part of the country. I refused and was made redundant. At my initial job interview, I had asked about the possibility of being made redundant because I had read the signs of recession in the news. They assured me that there was no possibility of this happening and convinced me that I was making a good career move. This came back to haunt them in the redundancy negotiations so they awarded me £2200 redundancy money and 10 weeks paid leave with continuing use of the company car to enable me to look for another job! I'd only been there 6 months but I was receiving as much as the employees who'd been there for 5 years. That was a fortune back in 1990 so I could relax after an amazing answered prayer. Even though I hated the job, I still gave it 100% and I feel I was rewarded for that. I stepped into another significant job because I now had the time to explore what I wanted to do next and I chose printing sales, which proved invaluable for the work I was doing at church. I had a blast before finishing in 1996 to have my son. I believe if we trust everything to God we can go further than we could ever dream of on our own.

3.   Fear of failure

I've covered this already in the first session but now, I also want to say that you are not going to succeed at everything you try. However, with small steps and changes, you can learn to adapt to the new circumstances you are in.

Give it a go

When James was 10 years old we bought him a small PlayStation toy that had limited access to the Internet. He'd got it to play games on but unbeknown to us, he had started to innocently search the web for other exciting toys. We didn't even know it was a feature of the machine. Imagine my shock when he came to me really excited to say he'd ordered something but didn't know how to pay. It was a Magnum 45, a real gun! He'd just been playing around pressing buttons without realising the dangers or understanding the consequences.

When we find ourselves feeling fearful, we don't always realise that we are actually getting into a position where our knowledge can expand. *Often the fear is unwarranted.* Fear magnifies in our minds and paralyses us: it stops us from having faith in ourselves and in God's will for our lives. It's at times like these that we need to rely on our gut feelings, arm ourselves with the right information and then move forward with confidence. Needless to say, we didn't order the gun and we put a stop to his web searches. But I remember at the time feeling a little frightened of using the web because I was worried I would press the wrong button or something and break the computer. I began to feel silly, and thought if a kid can do it, then so can I!

4. Fear of a NO

We all tend to be frightened of hearing a no. No to a bank loan; no you didn't get the job; no you haven't got a promotion or no to a sales call you made. Even though it may have been a business decision, we take it personally and it leaves us feeling inadequate. You can overcome these feelings by thinking differently about the word NO because although it's a negative, it can have a positive impact on your life. When *you* say no to someone it can mean a yes to yourself, especially if you are time poor.

In my early sales career, my boss gave me the best advice ever when he told me to always expect a no so that when I did hear it, it wouldn't bother me. So every day when we were trying to sell classified adverts in our local paper, we would have a fun game to see who was the *Top No Hearer.* From his years of experience, my boss knew about the law of averages and that approximately 25% of the sales calls would get a yes. It was a big numbers game and the more businesses you rang, the more yeses you would get and reach your target. Each time you got a no it was feedback which helped you to handle objections much more skilfully on the next call. I became a very successful salesperson and as my sales techniques improved, so did the yes statistics which went up to 50%. And my fear of cold-calling disappeared forever!

I still use this approach with everything in life – it can be very rewarding. It won't kill you if people say no and it can only dent your pride *if you let it.* Many companies know that people are afraid to take goods back and they push their 28-day returns policy knowing that very often, we'll just stick things in a cupboard because of the effort required to return them.

 Tony bought a pair of walkie-talkie watches for himself and James. I wasn't happy about it because I thought they were a waste of money – a passing fancy that would get used for a week and then forgotten about. That's exactly what happened. After 5 months they'd hardly been used so in February I decided they would be fun to use in Brownies for an evening walk. I was so cross when I discovered they weren't working. It was way past the return date and I couldn't find the receipt to try for a repair. Then 4 months later in June, I found the receipt and decided to try and get my money back. The worse they could say was no but it might be a yes! I deliberately chose a fairly young sales assistant rather than a senior member of staff. I smiled sweetly and explained my son's disappointment. Immediately, he asked if I would like £100 back in vouchers or the money put back on my card. Ohh the cash back please I beamed.

 **Visualise it going well**

When I went into the shop, I had already planned what I was going to say and the likely response but I had also *visualised* the assistant saying yes to my request. This helped me to feel relaxed and gave me the courage to carry out my plan. *So when you want things to go your way, visualise people saying yes to you.* Worrying isn't good for you but worrying *productively* can actually help to get you through anything – whether it's speaking in public or, in my case, taking those watches back to the shop. This *Mental Rehearsal Technique* is used by athletes, musicians, soldiers and even astronauts who use it to *prepare for the worst so that they can perform at their best.* The truth is that what we rehearse mentally, we tend to get. If you imagine going on stage and fluffing your lines in a play, hey presto, that's just what will happen. But if you do the groundwork beforehand and see yourself giving a smooth confident performance, that's what you're more likely to get. I tried this technique at a women's conference in a fun 10-minute spot called *laughology.* I'd never used this new material before and I was taking a risk because I was going to be asking the ladies to do some actions. In my mind, I *visualised* it going well and the ladies having a good laugh. This gave me the confidence to run with it and the results were exactly as I'd visualised.

I'll explain the science as best I can with an example. I think it's true to say that most of us feel a little nervous at the prospect of going to the dentist but some people suffer real fear and anxiety because they are *remembering* a previous bad experience. These emotions really kick in on the actual day and by the time you arrive at the dentist's, your nerves are in shreds. What we should be doing is playing that mini film in our mind of everything turning out as we want – no fillings today, feeling relaxed in the chair, keeping it all positive. Then when you get there, that's what the subconscious remembers and the nerves go away. Try it, it really does help. One lady told me she used this technique to overcome her fear of flying.

We can often spoil the whole day worrying about a 10-second smear test in the afternoon. I use the technique to remind myself that there is nothing to be afraid of because the discomfort will only last for a few seconds and I *visualise* the rest of the day going well. Sometimes we have to deal with challenging conversations like seeing our child's teacher about some bad behaviour in class. Learning to use this technique can help you to stay focussed and remain calm.

I wish I'd known about this approach when I had to tell a young girl she had body odour. I was a job placement officer but I couldn't get any employer to take her on because they could smell her in the interview. I made a right hash of it by trying to soften the bad news with saying something nice – I think I said her earrings were lovely and then told her she had BO! My execution was dreadful but she did take note and went on to get a full-time job. *Remember - any technique has to be practised before it will produce the right results.* **Visualisation is the biggest tool your brain has to help you succeed.**

We all have the ability. Just close your eyes and imagine your front door. See you did it. Smile whenever you are creating a positive scene in your head as it gives you a feel good boost. More science about that later.

5. Procrastination is the thief of time

Fewer than 7% of people do things right away so that means 93% of us put it off for another day. Like me not getting on with writing this because my Burmese cat came in for a stroke. I then went to feed her, saw the post had arrived, opened it, dealt with one of the letters, realised I'd not taken anything out of the freezer for tea and lo and behold, almost 45 minutes had passed since I typed the word thief!

In a relatively short time, America has become the world's richest and most successful country so what is it that sets it apart? Firstly, its latitude, climate, soil, arable land for cultivation and natural resources (iron, coal and oil) and secondly, there was lots of free land for settlers and open borders to attract immigrants from Europe. The promise of citizenship, rights and political participation also helped but the chance to make a fresh start and own your own land was a huge attraction. The early settlers from England and Ireland were the original *go getters.* They didn't want to struggle on over here putting up with a mediocre life. They *yearned* to achieve more, *saw the opportunities* that America had to offer and were prepared to take a risk. They fostered that *attitude and belief* into each subsequent generation until that winning mentality became second nature. They went with a dream and a plan and they practised success as part of their culture.

We often put things off because they seem overwhelming. I'm doing that right now; I should have rung the plumber about a leaking radiator 5 days ago so why haven't I? Because it's not a priority, but it may become one!

The secret is to break down the task into bite-sized chunks, *disassembling the biggest tasks to a manageable size.* 1% by 1% really comes into its own here. To do this you must adjust your thinking so, for example, if you've got to prepare the year's accounts, make your first task getting out the forms. Next day, find all the supporting paperwork and the day after, tot up a few sundries and expenses. Before you know it, you're half way completed and it didn't feel that overwhelming. The experts say that getting the most daunting task out of the way first makes everything else more achievable. We often leave that big one until last but then it hangs over us all the time like a dark cloud and puts us in rotten mood.

SO JUST GET ON WITH IT! I've got a great tool to share later that will help you do this.

Lack of effort can also be a problem

This can add days to a task and delay the fulfilment of your plan. At any time, we can *become forgetful and unfocussed*. It seems to be in us to take our time. Manufacturers have cottoned on to this form of procrastination. When Tony ran promotions on food packets, it was always easy to slow down the response by giving the entrant more to do. Short of asking for a piece of earlobe and a sample of DNA, just asking for the answers to be on a piece of paper 4" by 6" could delay a person entering the competition. In newspapers only 4% of our readership would ever enter so becoming a *comper*, as they are known in the competition world, actually gives you a higher chance of winning.

The art of goal setting

Research shows that setting a time frame for you to work at your goal is the key to a high success rate

Set yourself a specific date so that your progress is measurable. I was 13lbs overweight in the March with my 40th birthday looming in July. I couldn't fit into any of my favourite clothes and had developed 3 chins! I wanted to look fab at forty because I had planned a big party and didn't want to look overweight on the photos. I set myself a target of just 1lb per week, joined a gym and just started eating sensibly and exercising. Nothing drastic! I used the visualisation technique and saw myself looking slim and happy at my party. Week by week the pounds fell off and I felt encouraged because I was on target to be 8st 13lbs. I used the same technique for my 50th birthday losing 2 more pounds. I had an end date in mind and I could *measure the progress weekly* to see if I needed to change tactics.

To illustrate the tried and tested success of this technique, I produced the following goals sheet. You can see that not only did I set the goal but I also put the reasons I wanted to achieve it by the side. Remembering why I am working on something is very helpful in sticking to the plan. So far, I've achieved everything I've set out to do. One or two things had to change. My hubby has flatly refused to travel to the USA but has now kindly paid for a trip for James and I this year. We didn't go around the world on a cruise because we didn't realise James would become a successful child actor and needed to stay flexible whilst he wasn't independent. So that's something to look forward to. I'm not so sure I'll do the parachute jump this year though! These were just a few examples to show the Confidence Gym attendees and I then set a task for them to write down some of their own goals and put a time marker on them. I have a list to work to and each day it makes a difference to me knowing that I'm working towards something of value in my life.

My goals

YEAR	AGE	GOALS/AIMS	NOTES
2050	90	Live till i'm 90!	Keep a healthy lifestyle
2040	80	Travel in space	Keep healthy - save up
2030	70		
2025	65		Retirement - Pension kicks in
2020			
2019			
2018			
2017			
2016		Parachute jump	Keep healthy
2015			
2014		Still be under 10st	
2013			
2012		Around the world Cruise me, Tony & James	James left school - save up
2011		Paid off mortgage	
2010	50	Have a 50th Birthday Party Do a comedy routine	Start rehearsing Save up and book event
2009		Have my own career	
2008		Go to America Be confident on computer	Get Tony on short European flight 2007
2007 Aug- Dec		James right High School	Upgrade James maths
2007 Jan- July		Re-arrange House	A place for everything and everything in its place

I suggest you do a 5-year plan and then a yearly one to run alongside. Remember to write down your reasons for wanting to achieve your goal and anything else that will help you to keep on track. On the right of my 2010 goal was saving up. As I decided each month how much of my spare income to spend on myself; I remembered that the goal of paying off my mortgage would release a far wider spending plan. It worked and it also enabled Tony and I to fulfil a few lifetime yearnings.

A few pages on, you will find a set of topics to help you decide what areas of your life you would like to zing! Remember to look at the earlier set of questions you answered about the important things in life. These will help you develop a healthy mindset.

You will feel more positive in life when you have something to look forward to.

Right now at aged 55 I have a plan for my future. My main goal is to complete this book before the end of summer. I started out writing it as a pamphlet to give out at the end of each seminar but over the last 10 years, I've realised that I've gained so much knowledge and experience in confidence building, that it's become a book. The fact that you're reading it right now means I've already ticked it off and I will be on to the next exciting thing that keeps me positive about life. I've got space travel to look forward to in my 80s!

The best is yet to come

This statement has been a powerful mantra that has lifted me on many a dark morning when life hasn't turned out as I wished or I had bad news to deal with. *With God, the best is certainly yet to come.*

Remember the storybook I was going to write when I was 24? Well I was on holiday 10 years later in 1994 and woke up 4 nights in a row with a recurring dream. In these dreams, I had been on an adventure with my best childhood friend Pauline and as I awoke from each dream, we would be leaving an old-fashioned elevator, dressed in Victorian clothing. We were in a place that I later identified as Grand Central Station, New York but I'd never actually been there. I quickly scribbled down what I could remember and kept it safe until I got home.

I was working full-time so it wasn't until I fell pregnant with James in January 1996 that I found the time and the *desire* to write. It came very easily and I enjoyed it immensely. I wrote the first 9 chapters and then James was born in the August. Having a C-section meant a long recovery but by November I was back on track and I finished the book in April 1997. I prepared a synopsis, got the *Writers' and Artists' Yearbook* and sent it off to 6 publishers and BBC TV. I loved it so why wouldn't they? I got a polite letter back explaining that the transmission slot I'd suggested was for classic pieces of writing. I was so disappointed and after another 3 rejection letters and 2 that didn't even bother to reply, I put it on a shelf in my cupboard where it stayed for 15 years!

After doing this particular session at Confidence Gym, I thought I'd better put my own advice into practice and see if I could get my book published. I got it out but unfortunately the word processing programme I'd written it on was now obsolete so I had to retype all 40,000 words again! However, this enabled me to do some great editing. At the same time, I gave it out to some young readers and asked them if it was any good. They said it was but it needed a bit of work so I got some guidance from my friend's 12-year-old daughter Alice. I also had some adult readers who thought it was amazing and encouraged me to get it published. It was ready once again to send off but now I was in a different publishing era. Many authors were self-publishing on the web in a medium called *CreateSpace*. My friend Gillian Clarke who was proofreading it for me suggested that I let her son Graham upload it for me. In 2014 I held my published book with great pride, joy and excitement. It had taken 30 years but I'd done it at long last! My dream had become a reality. Available on Amazon my children's storybook *DRABACUS* for ages 8-12 can be bought as a kindle or paperback version. I learned so many things taking on that task so here are 2 I want to tell you about.

1. **Your resources are in your relationships** and I have been blessed to have the right people around me at the right time. In 1994 when my good friend Penny Higgins raved about my story, it was her excitement that encouraged me to go for it. And then there was Alice and Stacy who cheered me on and Gillian and Graham who offered their skills for very little money.

   Proverbs 25v11. The right word at the right time is like a custom made piece of jewellery. (The Message)

   My friend Jackie Dickinson offered to edit the book that you're reading now and I snapped her hand off!

2. **Along the way I've met so many new people** who have helped me to market and publish my books. I've been to interesting events and it's opened up a whole new exciting way of life. I've not got *set in my ways* as I was worried I would. *Just setting a few goals can launch you into a world of possibilities.* My children's novel is currently travelling the Seven Seas in the children's library onboard the Royal Caribbean ship *Anthem of the Seas.* Cool!

   How I've set a goal and timescale for this book

   So I know I can do this. I've done it before and it has built my confidence. I've identified people who can help. I've *written down* how I will benefit others from publishing all my findings. I've just got to set aside time, currently every afternoon, *and stick to it.* Complete bite-sized chunks everyday, and measure my progress by ticking off the task in my *To Do Book.* (Coming on to that shortly)

   Hey presto! Here we are with a dream and a plan in your hands!

   We are a do-it-yourself project

Research has shown that the winners in life are list makers. Achieving small goals bring self-esteem and confidence. Write a letter to make someone's day; try out a new recipe; take a different route home - you may even find it's quicker.

Remember that goals switch you on to a vibrant and exciting life.

 **When we see ourselves making progress it gives us a boost, which, in turn, helps us to feel in control**.

To do this effectively we need the <u>art of focus</u> in our lives - the skill of keeping stuff at the front of our minds so that we can *see opportunities* as they occur and take full advantage of them. I mentioned my *To Do Book* earlier so let me explain one of the best tools you can use to achieve goals and focus on what's important. The ladies who have been to this session tell me it's one of the best things they've taken from Confidence Gym.

 When James was born I found it hard to focus my mind on anything other than him. I was breastfeeding and because he wasn't a good sleeper, I was shattered all the time. I couldn't even remember which breast he'd last fed from. He was underweight so the midwife suggested that I should keep a record of his feeds, how much milk he'd taken and an R or L to remind me where I was up to. I got a little notebook and after a short time the midwife could see that he was now feeding properly. As I sat there feeding him, jobs that I needed to do would pop into my mind so I jotted them down at the back of the notebook. As I completed each task I went through it with a highlighter pen so that I could see it was done and dusted. <u>I noticed that this gave me a great sense of achievement</u>. I felt in control.

When James stopped breastfeeding 4 months later, I carried on with my little notebook. I'd realised that it was a fantastic *tool* because it was a rolling list and you

103

didn't have to write a new one each day. I started to use another page of the notebook to remind me about upcoming things such as renewing my insurance, buying a birthday card etc. At the back, I had a temperature record for James and details of any medication he was taking. Then I added a Christmas card and present list and a lending record to make sure I got books back! I created another section to cover projects I was involved in so that I could see at a glance, what I'd done and what still had to be completed. When all the tasks were grouped in this way, I could route plan my day. I became super efficient and never missed a thing just so long as I wrote it in my *To Do Book*! I don't even have to think about it now: *it's a habit.*

So many ladies have said it's transformed their lives. The great thing is that you can tailor it to suit you and how you go about things. Make it as in depth as you want. You can tear out the completed pages if you want but seeing what you've accomplished over the weeks, months and years can bring a real sense of achievement. I leave all my completed goals and tasks in there for this very reason. When Tony comes home and asks what I've been doing all day, I can just reel it all off! I've discovered there's nothing more satisfying than scrawling that highlighter pen through a completed task!

 *But you must keep your notebook handy or in the same place and look at it at least once a day.*

Here are the benefits at a glance.
1. You only write the task once.
2. See instantly what the priorities are.
3. Good for long term planning.
4. Group jobs together to target daily.
5. Route plan to save time on the road and save petrol.
6. See what you've already done.
7. Easy to see progress on certain jobs

All high achievers use their time well. A book that prioritises planning makes you highly effective so that you enjoy your day. But sometimes I have to confess that I've worn myself out trying to complete too much in one day so do be warned!

This tool may not be for you right now, or indeed ever. I've used it successfully for the last 20 years because it's part of my routine and I know it brings results to busy people.

Q Who do you know that may benefit from a good organisational tool? Let's share ideas. I know that there are now many apps on mobile phones etc that will even remind you when something needs doing. It's the same idea so just implement it.

Q What should I put in the book? If you were taken ill tomorrow, what would you need to tell someone else to do? That kind of covers it all – the rest is up to you.

Just *seeing all* the tasks you do, goals completed, big or small, can actually help you to get a real sense of your own value or worth. So often, we underestimate what we bring to family life. Many of you are looking after a partner, children or elderly relatives. If you're anything like me then you're also a cook, cleaner, holiday planner, accountant, nurse, trainer, entertainer, party organiser, teacher, advisor, taxi driver and confidant to name but a few. How many of these valuable skills do you take for granted? How often do you feel that your efforts go unnoticed?

Know who you are and be confident in it! Know your worth and act on it! You are brilliant!

For those of you who are ready to act, here's the goals suggestion list along with a template to complete.

Have fun and fulfil your destiny.

What kind of goals should I set?

Analyse where you really are now. **Be honest.**
For example, I'm not earning enough; I'm overweight; I feel lonely and want some company.

 **Determine** *how* **you will** *benefit* **from achieving your goal/s.**

Write it/them out **and then** *set a deadline* **for change.**

Identify groups or individuals that can help you.

You might want to think about the following areas:

Family
Are the children in good habits?
What do I need to do now to get them into the right school or a club they are interested in?
Do we need a new exciting meal plan?
Should we cut down on our TV watching?
Do we spend enough quality time together?

Personal achievements
Lose a stone in weight
Cut down on alcohol
Learn a foreign language
Write a novel

House
Do the garden up
Add an extension

Get a new kitchen
Move house

Holidays
Visit the USA, China – somewhere special
Spend time with overseas relatives
Try a cruise

Relationships
Get a partner
Go for counselling.
Improve family ties

Spiritual
Increase my prayer time
Start a ministry area
Discover a new spiritual gift

Career goals
Reduce my hours
Get a promotion
Change my job

Self-improvement
Do some self-development (you've started that already so well done!)
Get a new haircut
Change my makeup routine; it's out of date
Buy some new clothes

Financial goals
Save up for a new car
Pay off the mortgage earlier
Reduce the weekly shopping bill

Remember - a goal is not a wish.

YEAR	MY GOALS / AIMS	NOTES
2030		
2029		
2028		
2027		
2026		
2025		
2024		
2023		
2022		
2021		
2020		
2019		
2018		
2017		

Your Third Set
OF THINKING TOOLS

- What would your epitaph say?

- We all have an area of excellence.

- A goal switches you on to success.

- Every dream needs a plan.

- Achieving goals builds self-steem and confidence.

- Discover your passion.

- Whatever you hold in your mind you can accomplish.

- Don't fear what people think.

- Don't fear change or failure.

- Procrastination is the theif of time.

- See it going well.

- Your rescources are in your relationships.

- Set goals big and small.

- List makers are winners.

2

THE BEST IS YET TO COME!

Stress Busting

Stress kills confidence

We live in a world where stress comes at us from all directions but *what stresses one person stretches another*.

We need to think about stress to understand how it affects us. You've probably noticed that sometimes, being stressed motivates you to focus on your work, yet at other times, you feel overwhelmed and unable to concentrate on anything. While stress affects everyone in different ways, there are 2 main types: stress that's beneficial and motivating (good stress) and stress that causes anxiety and health problems (bad stress).

We also rejoice in our sufferings, because we know that suffering produces perseverance, perseverance, character, and character, hope.

Romans 5 v3&4 (NIV 1984)

The Confidence Gym logo is a butterfly. Here is a story that I think fits in well. A guy was watching a butterfly emerging from its cocoon. This stage of its life occurs after it has been a caterpillar and it begins to pupate in order to transform into a butterfly. As he watched it struggle, he became frustrated at the amount of time it was taking to escape so he decided to help it along by snipping the cocoon open with some scissors. The butterfly emerged quickly but to his surprise, it had a swollen body and small, shrivelled wings. He thought that any minute, the wings would enlarge and expand to enable it to fly but, nothing happened. It fell to the ground, never to recover. What he had not understood was that the butterfly was supposed to *struggle* its way out of the cocoon so that vital liquids would shoot into the veins in the wings, allowing them to open in readiness for flight. Without this struggle, the butterfly would never be able to fly.

Struggle is an important part of any growth experience - it is the struggle that enables you to develop your ability to fly.
My aim for you is that you fly with stronger wings.

As I look back at my life, I realise that my greatest struggles have produced some of my best moments. Although painful at the time, it has built a valuable platform which has increased my life experience bringing many rewards e.g. giving birth!

First of all, I want to say that looking at ways to combat stress can often be about replenishing our tank to keep the flow going.

 **Know what fills your tank and what drains it.**

If we are depleted, then there's no energy to give out.

Fillers
Reading, Laughing, Serving, Friends, Family time, Shopping, Holidays, Exercise, Hobbies, Food pleasures.
Drainers.
Too taxing a schedule, Toxic friends, Too many friends, Work conflicts, Family arguments.

Our emotional resilience needs to be built up so that we have a protective force field around to bat away the things that come at us. One of the things we can do to maintain this is to keep learning, just as you are now:

- Having a good life balance is essential.
- Planning times of refreshment *before* you get busy is a sensible approach that bears fruit.
- Putting the important people/things first and making sure everything works around this is key.

Too many people, (Dads especially) put work first allowing relationships at home to suffer and become malnourished, leading to family breakups. A friend of mine recognised that this was affecting his home life and took action. At the *start* of the year, he decided when he and his family would have their main 2-week holiday and he also factored in plenty of days off around weekends and single days off. He also arranged to adjust his work hours so that he could do the school run. His wife said their home life was turned around with this forward planning, creating much less stress. I asked my husband Tony if he would consider doing the same as for many years he had not taken his holidays. This impacted on our son more than me. However, because of the nature of his work it became too difficult for him but this may not be the case for you and your family.

It really comes down to priorities in life. Decide what they are and stick to them.

 **Q** Think now, what are the top 3 priorities in your life?

Everybody's will be different, but remembering that <u>people</u> are more important than things can help put your mind on the right track. Too many families have split up because someone wanted a career and all the external trappings of success.

Don't be fooled by the pressure of providing well for your family, research shows that children just want to grow up in a loving home.

My life changed when I became a mother. I'd lived a pretty stress-free life up until then except for the anxiety of wondering whether I would ever be a mum as it took 15 years for me to get pregnant. My face was unlined, my hair wasn't going gray and I always got a good night's sleep. What a shocker it is when all this changes so dramatically. I never tell first-time mums what's in store for them as they'll find out soon enough! Besides some babies are good sleepers (mine wasn't) and some dads are very hands on.

You've got to work with your Model. *(Cath Stanley. New wives club 2014)*

Lack of sleep was affecting me badly. I could barely think straight so I had to put up some basic charts and lists (covered earlier in Session 2) in order to *cope*. Thank goodness for both sets of parents stepping in and giving me some breathing space and time to rest. I wasn't afraid to ask for help - I'm no martyr, just soldiering on – I grabbed what was offered.

If I hadn't *recognised* the need to get some *me time*, I would have sunk to the bottom and been no help to my husband and son. We do have a responsibility to help ourselves.

Here are some simple refreshers that have worked for me and other chums.

- A coffee with upbeat, positive friends.
- A walk in the woods or countryside. Just 30 minutes can do the trick.
- Someone else cooking a meal for you.
- Things that combine friendship and exercise. Maybe a short run together. Or gym and swim nights - that's what me and my friend Debs used to do. It's the best combo ever, chat and workout!

Research shows that exercise can aid healing in your mind on an incredible scale. I'm not covering this right now (there's lots of information online if you Google it) but having seen the research, I do know that *exercise has a huge impact on our health and general well-being and in fighting depression*.

The biggest killer in the world is your armchair! We were designed to move every hour or so to get your lymphatic systems circulating through the whole body. If you work at a desk for 8 hours a day as I do on a Friday, it's recommended that you get up for 5 minutes every hour. Thankfully my desk is on reception, not an area shared with anybody else, so when no one's looking, I'll get up and do some dancing or star jumps for 30 seconds, stretching, running on the spot, even a good body shake!

My husband's work is very stressful so he comes home shattered every weekday. He's always yawning as he flops into his chair to watch a film. No matter how many times I tell him that exercise will revive him, he's having none of it. However, the stress chemicals that keep you going at work turn into a wind-down wash of tiredness as a pay off for all that *get going juice* during the day. More of that in the science section later. When you feel tired the last thing you want to do is physical exercise but it's a *mind over matter skill* that can energise you. When I do manage to persuade Tony to have a brisk walk for 10 minutes, he always comes back feeling refreshed. If he could overcome the *habit* of chilling in front of the TV in the *belief* that this will rest him, I think he'd be happier.

Stress hormones versus relaxing hormones

Sharing helps too

Finding out that you can do something quicker, more efficiently or make a saving etc. is very satisfying indeed.

Research shows that when we collaborate to improve our lives, it releases good hormones into your system that give you a boost. We girls are really good at sharing tips with each other. My *Top Ten Tips* DVD was born out of the story I told you about being a perfect housewife. Now I'm not talking *Stepford Wives* here but the benefits are really positive for the giver and the receiver. Aren't you just buzzing when you discover something new or solve a problem you were having?

So how about arranging a Top Tips night? Each person shares 3 labour saving things they've found that improve their lives. You can have demonstrations, video clips from the web, and then all vote to see which one is best. Everyone learns something and if they are a 5%er and put into action what they've learned, then it's a win-win night.

But do be careful not to share *gossip* as this injects negativity into the mix. It's fine to tell a friend of someone's plight but resist putting your *judgement* on it. After all, it's none of your business. I can remember leaving some girlfriends' houses feeling quite sick with everything they'd spewed over me about other people. Later I will explain <u>why</u> this is *harmful* to you and your relationships.

Gossips can't keep secrets, so never confide in blabbermouths
Proverbs 20 v19. (The Message)

Why don't you consider performing this exercise?
List all the people (and it's not just women!) that:
a) Are prone to gossip.
b) Leave you feeling empowered.

The next step is to avoid those in the first group - seriously!

It's tough and I've done this at least twice in the last 8 years because I recognised their dampening effect upon me. Actually, they drew out my true feelings and got me involved in unpleasant conversations that I wished had never got started. Stepping back from such situations takes wisdom and courage but it's important to surround yourself with positive people who are cheering you on instead of *pulling you down*.

Horror of horrors, *you* may be this negative person. It won't do you any harm to think about your conversations and admit that you shouldn't have judged so and so. When you read the science later on, I hope you are encouraged to rethink your criticism.

Our confidence is robbed when we don't feel in control.

Loss of memory is a confidence stealer.

When I was pregnant with James I became so forgetful. This is a short-term memory loss known as *baby brain syndrome*. Research suggests that women's brains change during pregnancy so that they will be better able to concentrate on their newborn's needs after the birth, with the result that they become less focused on other things, such as where the car keys are. During pregnancy, increased oestrogen levels kick-start the neurons in the brain which then multiply at the rate of 250,000 a minute to prepare you for the demands of motherhood (like surviving on 2 hours sleep a day!). This is the brain's way of retuning itself to meet your needs.

Neuroplasticity (a word we heard in Session 1) is the brain's ability to reorganise itself by forming new connections in the hippocampus, the brain's memory centre. That's why you can become forgetful as new behaviours of feeding and protecting come into play. We've all heard the jokes about women becoming stupid so it's reassuring when you know that it's all part of the process. And we all know of women who we thought would never make good mothers but who completely transform in time for the baby, just as they've been biologically programmed to do.

My memory isn't as good as it was but I put that down to the ageing process. I've found it essential to develop some tools and techniques to improve it and I don't know how I would cope without my *TO DO BOOK*. This is mentioned in Session 2 so if you've skipped that session, go back and have a look because the idea started when my baby brain appeared.

Here are some *tried and tested techniques* to improve your memory in your everyday life. Habits you can get into that will diminish thoughts like:

- Did I lock the door?

118

- Did I turn off that pan of potatoes?
- Have I fed the cat?

I've lost count of the number of times I've had to reverse down my road back to the house to check on such niggles!

The door *is* always locked, apart from once, but that's a story for another time.

As you leave your house, your mind is so full of where you're going and what you're going to do, that you're on autopilot. It's when you switch to normal focusing and thinking that you start to wonder whether you've turned the iron off!

Solutions that work

These are *habits* that you will have to work on before they become second nature.

Starting with locking things. As you press the button or turn the key, *say out loud*, 'I've locked and I've knocked' *knocking* with your knuckle as you say the last bit. Saying it out loud and performing an action, marks it in your brain. *This works.*

After experiencing 3 dried out pans of stew, 1 exploded boiled egg all over the ceiling and the start of a pan fire, I really had to take action! As a prompt, you place your car keys by the stove. When you're ready to leave you have to collect them and this prompts you to check the stove. Then *say out loud*, 'It's off, off, off' while *banging* your fist on the worktop at the same time. Then, when you're half a mile away and get the dreaded thought, your throbbing hand will remind you that all is well. *This works.*

A word of warning though. Once you are in the habit, you start to become confident very quickly and you may find that you start missing out one of the steps. This technique will only work if you perform both of them - just being honest!

3

Same goes for when you park the car. If you're like me and don't want it pranged, you park right at the far end of the car park to avoid the twerp who just flings his door open without a thought. You set off walking and then you wonder whether you've locked it. And that is the start of your long trek all the way back frantically pressing the key fob until it picks up a signal!

I was visiting my uncle in hospital and Tony told me to be careful not to leave any items on view in the car as there'd been a spate of break-ins on the hospital car park. When I arrived, I dutifully moved everything into the boot but just as I walked into the hospital, I suddenly thought, 'Did I lock the car?' Groaning out loud, I turned around to walk back and saw that I had left my tailgate high in the air for all to see! I had locked the doors though!

So my next tip is to *look back* as you leave an area. If I'd done this at the gym, I wouldn't have lost 2 swimsuits, 5 bottles of shampoo and a lock! I *say out loud,* 'Look back' and sometimes I even sing it to the tune of that Beatles' song *Get Back*. It's actually more fun singing and folks don't look at me strangely. I was pleased to hear from a life coach I know that she adopts the same approach but calls it the stupid look!

A place for everything and everything in its place

It's said that we lose up to 16 minutes a day looking for about 9 misplaced items. I can admit to a couple of hours a week though some of the time, I don't really look properly. It's so infuriating when Tony finds the item in a place that I'm supposed to have already searched – it's the smug look that gets me. So in an attempt to get less of those looks, I have endeavoured to have a place for every item in the house. It's harder than you think when you *try* to put it into practice. Again, it's down to a *habit* of *always* putting it in the right place.

On my very first Confidence Gym at Farington Lodge, Leyland I decided to arrive an hour early to set up so that I would be relaxed as everyone arrived. I had my coat on all ready to leave home but my glasses were nowhere to be found. I can't see a thing without them so Tony and James started searching only for me to find them 35 minutes later on Tony's pillow. I'd taken them off and put them in a place they would *never normally* go. By this time, I was running late and totally stressed out - I drove to the venue like a bat on speed! I had to come up with an action plan so that this would never happen again. First of all, I ordered a spare pair and then I came up with an idea that's sheer genius and means I don't spend a second looking for those glasses anymore. If I can't find them, I go straight to my cupboard where the spare is kept, put them on and go about my business. Hey presto, before long I come across the lost glasses which I just put back in the cupboard. It's saved me hours over the last few months. I did try wearing them on a spectacles chain but got all tangled up in them, and someone said I looked like their great-grandma!

Always have a plan to fall back on.

Remembering things as you are going to sleep

If you get a eureka moment when you're in bed thinking over the day's events and planning tomorrow, you can pick up your mobile from the side of the bed and set a reminder. However, research about blue-light emissions from mobiles suggests that they suppress the sleep hormone melatonin and thus, cause sleep problems. Not good! So here's a better idea that works for me if I need to remember to do something first thing. I put an item in an unusual or different place e.g. a sock on top of the radio on my bedside table. As soon as I see it in the morning, it triggers my memory. Occasionally, I've seen the sock and not been able to remember what it's there for but it always comes to me later in the morning because I know that there is *something to remember.*

You might be wondering why I don't just write myself a note. Well that's what I do if I've not turned the light out. I'm talking about the stuff that you've not had time to do like putting a wash on before you go out. Chuck a dishcloth on the kitchen floor to remind you to do it when you come back in. Something out of place can be a great *trigger* for your memory unless, of course, you live in a very untidy house!

Here's a good set of rules which can alleviate bedtime worrying. Categorise the thought into one of three areas.

1. *Do it.* It could be that noise downstairs or wondering whether your keys are out of reach of a thief. Get out of bed and sort it out. Just do it.

2. *Plan it.* If you think of the best money-saving tip in the world, the chances are that you won't remember it in the morning so get your notebook out and write it down.

3. *Forget it.* If it's something you can't action right away, put it to bed as well and *say*, 'I forget you.'

<u>If you're driving</u> and you think of something, then breathe on your door window and write in the mist with your finger. It will magically appear when you breathe on it again. I've just remembered why I carried a microfibre cloth for years in the side pocket - to wipe all the scribbles off! Now I shout to my phone and Siri will put a reminder in my notes. (Siri is a voice-controlled personal assistant available on iPhones).

Singing it

Imagine that you're in the car and you realise that you need to get some shopping. It's so annoying to get home after you've shopped only to find that you've forgotten something. I think of the things I need and then put them into a song and amazingly, when I get into the shop, my song delivers every item. In the Confidence Gym session, I demonstrate by presenting each table with a list of items. They have to come up with a song and sing it out to the whole room. Oh, we get actions and everything! The secret is to use a tune you are familiar with and some of the best songs I've heard were set to nursery rhymes - Frères Jacques is particularly good. Try it with this list.

Peas and carrots,
Peas and carrots,
Bisto too, Bisto too,
Add a drop of lemon, eat a ripe banana, chocolates too, chocolates too.

You never forget advertising jingles like *Beanz Meanz Heinz* so use something familiar like this to help you with the unfamiliar.

Another tip is to remember *how many* items you have to buy. Make a point of saying, 'It's 6 things I need' and that will focus your mind to remember 6 items.

These ideas may seem bonkers to you but *they do work*.

By taking control, your confidence in your ability will grow.

We never lose it

One of the best things we can do for ourselves is to memorise Scripture so that we can recall our Lord's promises for our lives *right when we need that reassurance*. We have been designed to rely on His word - it's a power line – but we don't always draw on it.

One of the best times to learn is when we are *young.* You don't lose the old memories as you age, just the new ones, because your ability to record them gradually wears out. That's why we forget what we've gone into a room for but we can still remember our phone number from 40 years ago. Darwen 76695 was mine and I don't even need to think about it!

So, armed with this knowledge that we can be comforted by promise after promise unto old age, encourage the small children in your life to commit

123

these promises to memory now. Put a post-it note by their bed, or on the computer screen, give them a heads up now which will be a gift forever.

Train up a child in the way he should go, and when he is old he will not depart from it.

(Proverbs 22:6 New King James Version)

Best practice at stress reduction

Stress is mainly the end product of negative thinking but not all stress is bad as some people thrive under it.

Much of the stress that we experience is self-generated. It can be created by our hectic schedules or feelings of helplessness when we are faced with a situation that we are *used* to controlling.

 ***But the more often you are hit with something, the more you can handle it by learning from the experience.***

James and I have just watched a TV programme about the SAS selection process. It was pretty tough and there was something they did right at the end that I couldn't understand. After a brutal endurance test, the few remaining candidates were sent off on a hunt. They were the prey and had to avoid capture. Of course, they were all captured and they then had to undergo a mock interrogation. Imitating a real-life interrogation, they were made to wear bags over their heads, roughly handled and mentally tortured until all but 2 gave in. The officers said they do this exercise because when you know what to expect it can *inoculate* you to the *shock* of capture, maintain lower stress levels and control your mind to follow a carefully managed process of keeping your mouth shut. This is called *Stress Inoculation Training*, a psychotherapy method intended to help people prepare themselves in advance to handle *stressful* events successfully and with the minimum of upset. So if this works in a real warfare situation, let's give it a go!

If you fall to pieces in a crisis then there wasn't much to you in the first place.
Proverbs 24 v10. (The Message)

It is also a biblical principle. When King David took on the giant warrior Goliath he wasn't frightened of him. He had already fought off lions and bears to protect his father's sheep. He was mentally prepared - he knew the

3

feelings he would experience and he didn't let it faze him, knocking Goliath for a six!

Common triggers of stress

We hear or see something and it preys on our mind - we think the worst because that is often our default setting (as we learned in Session 1). This story is a good one to ponder.

Jim was always borrowing things from his neighbour Harry and now he wanted to borrow his lawnmower. As he set off to Harry's house his mind was filled with thoughts. 'He probably won't want to lend it to me because I didn't let him borrow my best spade the other week. I bet he says it's at his sister's house. Well, if he does, I'll offer to go and get it. If he comes up with another excuse like it needs sharpening, I'll offer to fix it.' He arrived at Harry's door and knocked forcefully. As soon as Harry opened it, Jim blurted out, 'D'you know what, you can stuff your lawnmower!' When I heard this story I laughed my head off as does everyone on the course. Let's be honest, we've all had our Jim moments haven't we?!

 We must learn to *recognise negative self-talk quickly* and boot it out of our minds when it's not a true threat. We often entertain negative thoughts with *no evidence, guesswork* or *little foundation*. In other words, we are *mind reading.* The *problem* comes when we come face to face with the person as Jim did with Harry. *We subconsciously treat them as if they've been part of the earlier conversation.*

Our attitude is in *negative mode* and we are *not receptive to reality.* The other person can pick up on this and the relationship may start to deteriorate.

 A lady came up to me after she had attended this session of Confidence Gym. She had recognised her wrong thinking and asked me to forgive her for blanking me at a relative's funeral 10 years earlier. I

126

had no recollection of the incident and I felt dreadfully sorry for her. For so long, she'd had these thoughts of offending me when I had absolutely no idea she was in such turmoil. I reassured her that her mind reading was a figment of her own imagination and she breathed a sigh of relief that the burden was lifted.

On another occasion, a guy at church came to speak to me after a sermon on forgiveness. He said he'd held a grudge against me for 3 years. Apparently, I had asked him to help unload a lorry but without me knowing, someone else had done it instead. This guy took offence because he wrongly concluded that I thought he was incompetent and had sought help from someone better qualified. It was unloading a lorry for goodness sake! I don't know what insecurities he was carrying but this incident had just triggered something in him. But the point is that for 3 years, I'd had no clue about his feelings and I hadn't noticed anything awkward in his attitude towards me. If guilt has made you think that you should apologise, I would always test the situation first to see if the other person *has* even noticed your cooler behaviour in the first place. So if it's all in your head - keep it to yourself and don't create a problem where there really isn't one!

I've gone on about this because bad communication is the start to relationship breakdown.

We need to check out the situation before we get all hot and bothered thinking we have upset someone. Listen to this story and you'll see what I mean.

I was driving to church with James who suddenly said he felt sick. I speeded up only to get stuck behind a Sunday driver doing 20 miles an hour in a 30 zone. Eventually, I managed to overtake on the dual carriageway but in my haste and frustration, I did cut in front rather badly probably forcing them to break hard. To my horror, as I indicated to drive into the church car park, so did they! And to make matters worse, it was my friend Christine. She glared at me as she helped her elderly mum and father-in-law out the car. I felt so embarrassed and as soon as I had sorted James out, I rushed over to apologise. I thought she would give me a real blasting but guess what - she didn't know what I was talking about and hadn't even noticed me cut in front of her! She said, 'Oh Su, I'm in a total daydream when I'm driving. I never even saw you.' We both laughed at my wrongly interpreting her glare as a telling off when it was actually her getting impatient waiting for her relatives to get out the car!

Don't jump to conclusions – there may be a perfectly good explanation for what you just saw.
Proverbs 25 v 8 (The Message)

So talk first before launching into an unnecessary apology and do it sooner rather than later.

We all need an eye test

You've heard the expression, looking through rose-tinted glasses. This is when we have an optimistic, positive perception of something (or somebody) often thinking of it as better than it actually is. But I'd like to suggest that we all look at people through glasses that we don't even realise we're wearing!

As time passes, we form opinions of our friends and work colleagues based on the experiences we have shared. One time, a lad was late for work and got a right telling off from the boss. Moments later, someone else arrived late but nothing was said because the boss liked him. He had taken his glasses off for this person: they were both late but the tolerance level had dropped over time for the first lad.

Even our families are not immune and if we aren't careful, relationships can break down. The little irritating things they do, like not putting the top back on the toothpaste, can start to *create a lens*. We then view everything they say, see and do through filters of:

- They don't care about me.
- They are always trying to avoid work.
- They don't like me.
- They are stingy.
- They are stupid and useless.

What happens in our minds is that we don't hear something as it is *actually* being presented but rather, by *how we want to interpret it.* In other words, we are judging without viewing all the sides properly.

 ***Do you need to order a new pair of specs?***

You'll also remember from Session 1 that we often take a negative view of people who don't behave or think in the same way as us.

So we end up focusing on the wrong things when we should be seeing clearly.

Q Do you know one person in the world who is right about everything? Have a good think. The answer is always going to be *NO.*

So this means that *all of us are going to be wrong some of the time.*

It takes courage and humility to realise that *you* may be exacerbating a situation. We hate to admit we are in the wrong but someone is! Sometimes, we're just too stubborn or proud to admit it but the first person to say, 'Hey, I'm sorry. I got it wrong' is the one who takes the heat out of the situation, reduces stress levels and clears the way for clarity and harmony.

That's why I love mediation. It doesn't need to be done by a professional - your friends are often the best

129

choice because they can see both sides and don't have any emotional involvement.

When you are emotional, you are not rational.

 Take time now to have your eye examination and think about these questions.

Q What glasses do I wear and for whom?

Q Am I wearing contact lenses that prevent others from seeing my feelings and thus making it difficult to resolve the issue?

(Remember that we are aiming to have fulfilling relationships).

Q What do others see when they hear me? Am I actually wrong about something?

Q Should I change my tone of voice?

(Sometimes, the way we say things is more hurtful than what we are saying).

I'm not offering a complete solution here because I don't have that level of expertise. But I want you to see that unwittingly, we behave in a way that increases our stress level and makes the problem worse by failing to address it.

Offence

The Bible confirms that we will all experience feeling offended. You don't know when it's going to come and in what form. I've been upset this year at a friend who never thanked me for an expensive gift. I would have written a card, texted or phoned but again, *I'm expecting someone else to behave like me.* It's been tough to forget it but now I have done so and my joy has been restored.

It's easy to take offence at what someone has done to you but it can also create other problems.

 This is a story told by Joel Osteen, the Senior Pastor of Lakewood Church, Houston, Texas. He had flown across America to preach in Los Angeles. On arrival, he took a taxi and got a book out to read. When he hadn't reached his destination when he expected to Joel thought to himself, 'This driver thinks I'm a tourist who doesn't know the quickest way to the church but I do!' When Joel challenged the driver he explained that he avoided the direct route because, 'There's a guy who lives down that road who has wronged me so I can't even stand to drive past his house. It gives me a bad feeling.' Joel held his tongue but thought to himself, 'Well that's ok for you, but everyone else is *paying the price of your bitterness* with a higher taxi fare!'

When I'm with someone who has a problem with another person, it can affect what you want to accomplish or make things really awkward as you navigate your way around the ill feeling. Our negativity gets stored inside us and turns into unforgiveness which then poisons our body.

You will probably have heard these wise sayings.

Holding onto anger is like drinking poison and expecting the other person to die.

We become a prisoner to our thoughts, unable to operate freely because of the barriers we have put up. It is *self-destructive*.

The key to the prison is hanging up by the door, the handle on the inside.

Familiarity breeds contempt

Families can be very fragile and I know quite a few people who never speak to their close relatives and siblings. The family relationship has fractured.

It can be very hurtful when those closest to us think that this gives them the *right* to tell us a few home truths. This is often done under the pretext of wanting the *best* for you. Twice in the past, Tony and I have fallen victim to this with close friends and it culminated with us falling out with them. These experiences were so painful that we intentionally avoided developing new friendships for fear of a repeat performance. We now know how to handle this so it's not an issue any more. (And we made up with our friends).

 My grandma often used to tell me that I had a fat face or my hair was a mess and my fringe too long. Every time we visited her, we used to wonder what critical comments she would come out with. The truth is I did have a fat face on one visit and I was a little overweight (it always goes on my chin first of all!). Now that grandma is no longer around, my mother has taken on her role. Are they being cruel to be kind? In their view yes, they want the best for me. But *the way it's said* can often deliver the killer blow but thankfully, in my case, it was always said in a nice way.

Only the other week, my aunty, my grandma's daughter, told me to hold my back straight because I was stooping. She then hunched herself over to show me how bad I looked. It certainly hit home. She was worried she had offended me but I love the fact that she wants the *best for me*, to stop something before it becomes irreversible. I think this *tell it straight* gene must run in my family because Tony tells me I sometimes say things that are inappropriate but to me, I'm loving someone to the extent that I'm willing to sacrifice my relationship. Thankfully, I can't think of anyone that I have an awkward relationship with but perhaps they're just not telling me!

Worry produces stress

Psychologists define worry as the negative thoughts, images and emotions in which mental attempts are made to avoid anticipated potential threats. Worry is experienced as feelings of anxiety about real or imagined issues, often personal in nature.

When we worry, we dwell on a negative situation and feel powerless to do anything about it. It seems to hound you as your *mind runs riot.*

One day I caught a whiff of damp in my kitchen and immediately, I remembered a comment from one of the neighbours that there was a natural spring under our newly-built house. Obviously, this was very worrying but when I checked with the builder, he thought it unlikely but couldn't give me a definitive answer because in truth, he didn't know for sure. I then asked a neighbour who had lived in the area for years and knew it really well. He reassured me that my other neighbour didn't know what she was talking about, it was nonsense and she was just scaremongering. But now as I smelt damp, I wondered whether she was right after all. I looked high and low for leaks in the floor, walls and ceilings. Then I imagined the work that would be involved if they had to dig under the floor to cap the spring off and redirect the water. For 2 days it preyed on my mind and I was thoroughly miserable and agitated. I was kicking myself for not having taken things further with the builder when I had the chance. Just as I decided that I would ring him, Tony walked into the kitchen and said, 'Isn't it about time you got rid of those old flowers? They're beginning to stink!' I went over to them and as soon as I took a sniff, I felt like shouting with joy - the damp smell was coming from them! I didn't let on to Tony because if he'd found out what I'd been putting myself through, he'd have had no sympathy. The answer had literally been right under my nose all along. All that stress and worry for nothing!

I know how to combat negative thoughts (I cover it in Session 1) so it bothered me that in the previous situation, I had allowed my neighbour's comment to distract me from the truth. So now, I have another great strategy to share and you will see how it can be applied to my smelly old flowers tale as we go through it together.

Can I remind you that *90% of what we worry about never happens?*

For further reading, I recommend a brilliant book by Dr Sarah Edelman *Change Your Thinking with CBT: Overcome Stress, Combat Anxiety and Improve Your Life.* Her book is a practical and supportive guide which shows you how to use CBT (cognitive behavioural therapy) techniques to overcome self-defeating thoughts and behaviours. Primarily, CBT uses the Socratic Method from the ancient Greek philosopher Socrates. When people were faced with a worry or dilemma, he would ask them a series of questions as a way of gradually helping them to realise that their worries and concerns may be irrational and nonsensical. This method puts the problem into perspective thereby enabling you to decide how serious it is and whether you are justified in worrying about it.

 **When we are in a highly anxious state, we don't think straight.**

Dr Edelman says that we selectively focus on our feared situations, overestimate the likelihood of worst case scenarios and predict catastrophic consequences. In other words, all the things I did when I sniffed the damp in the kitchen! In my case, at the time of discovering the damp problem, the questions and answers would have gone like this:

Q Describe the situation you are worried about?

A *I'm worried my house is sitting on a natural spring.*

Q Specifically, what do you fear might happen?

A *Water will seep through the floor and eventually flood my house.*

Q On a scale of 1 – 100, how likely is this to happen?

A *75 in my present state of mind.*

Q. What evidence supports your worrying thoughts?

A *I can smell damp in the kitchen.*

Q If it did happen, what action could you take?

A *I could go and live in a caravan in the garden until it was sorted out.*

Q Realistically, what's the worst thing that could happen?

A *Our house will be damp forever and that would knock thousands of pounds off the value.*

Q What's the best thing that could happen?

A *I find out that it's some old flowers sitting in smelly water.*

Q What's the most likely thing that could happen?

A *It will be something and nothing.*

Q Are there any actions you can take now?

A *I can ring the builder to ask about the foundation work.*

Q What would you tell a friend in the same situation?

A *They were overreacting to the problem before they had all the facts/Buy a boat!*

Q On a scale of 1 – 100, now re-rate the likelihood that your fears will be realized.

A *30.*

This process gradually calms you down.

Another calming exercise you can do when you feel as if your brain is bursting with worries, is to *write them down*. This releases them from your mind and you will feel less tense and anxious. When they're in black and white, they stay on the page.

My first instinct is to pray about everything but with the damp situation, I did let my *imagination run riot* and I suffered the consequences of not applying a little knowledge and common sense. Not a 5%er on this occasion!

Ultimately, I know God will turn to my advantage anything that gets in my way and, when I look back, I can see that many of my disappointments have been *His appointments*. When you really get a hold of this fact, you can rest in his assurance.

Another question to ask yourself is, '*Will this* matter *next week, next year or in 5 years' time?*' This can be a good worry leveller as you realise that many things won't matter at the end of the day!

The aim of this whole session is to *eliminate* as much stress as possible and thereby enable you to become more confident. Learn to handle stress well and your life experience will improve.

Problems are inevitable but misery is optional

Using coping statements can be very effective in managing what comes at you and in developing a more positive approach. They are truthful positive statements used to replace the negative and untrue thoughts that take over when you feel anxious, stressed and overwhelmed. For example, you can replace, '*I can't take this anymore.*' with, '*This is uncomfortable, but I can handle it if I take slow and deep breaths.*'

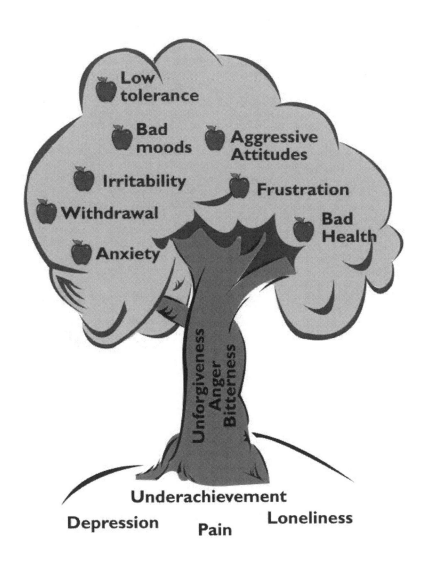

Excess stress and worry makes you ill

In my worry tree illustration, you can see the roots at the bottom - *depression, pain and loneliness.*

I've just heard on the radio that loneliness is as bad for you as smoking 15 cigarettes a day! (Taken from research conducted by Holt-Lunstad 2010 Social Relationships and Mortality Risk).

Underachievement is also on there, that's why it's so important to make your life worthwhile and purposeful as I've talked about in Session 2.

These feelings turn into attitudes, some of which are also shown on the bark of the tree - *unforgiveness, anger and bitterness.*

Do you see what happens though? They turn out to be fruit in your life.

Look at the apples – do you recognise any of those in your life?

In the last 20 years, science has been able to tell us what happens physically when stress hormones enter our system. An excellent book for further study is *Deadly Emotions: Understand the Mind-Body-Spirit Connection That Can Heal or Destroy You* by Dr Don Colbert. The book explains what is happening to our bodies when we are under stress and provides hints on how to change the damaging effects of our thoughts and emotions.

Research has also shown that a significant percentage of *disease* in the body is caused by *dis-ease* of the soul, which is made up of your *mind, will and emotions.*

- Over 75% of GP visits are stress related.
- A third of people regularly wake up several times a night with worry.

- Consultations with professionals uncover causes of *painful memories, hurtful words and unforgiveness towards others.*

Conclusion
What you feel emotionally becomes how you feel physically.
Remember this from Session 1?
The gardener (you) planting shrubs or weeds.
The captain (you) giving good or bad orders

Note this important fact
Every time you recall an event in your mind you are also *downloading* an *emotion*, rather like an attachment in an email. You can try this out right now. Just think of a sad time and it won't be long before you have a tear in your eye. If I sing the title tune of the film *Superman*, I start to feel euphoric at this hero in our world and then I cry with joy!

That emotion then has the power to flood your body with stress chemicals *as if the event is happening all over again right now.*

It's like having a scab that's still healing: if you pick it, it will bleed again. We all know people who love to show you their scabs - they want you to see what they've been through. They want a pity party and you're the invited guest. Make sure you don't throw any yourself.

Here are the adverse effects on your body

- **Weight gain to the middle.**

- **Salt retention**

- **Raises insulin & cholesterol.**

- **Impairs the immune system.**

140

- **Memory loss & learning ability.**

- **Decrease in bone density.**

- **Psoriasis & Eczema.**

- **Links to Allergies.**

- **Increased risk of cancer**

Ready to chew? It's a science bit.

The brain sends signals to our body's organs via neurons which are messenger cells in the nervous system, a bio chemical code. The neurons release various different chemicals called neurotransmitters that facilitate the transmission of nerve impulses. Each neurotransmitter is coded to perform a particular function, for example, acetylcholine which stimulates the skeletal muscles. (Study more from Dr Colbert's book if you wish).

Adrenaline is the key hormone for the *fight-or-flight* stress response. When it enters the bloodstream, it increases oxygen and glucose to the brain and muscles thus giving us the energy to respond quickly to an emergency situation, like being chased by an angry bull! That adrenaline boost allows us to run away much faster than normal. It can be a life saver.

However, the downside is that after the adrenaline surge it is common to feel quite weak and tired. This is down to falling blood sugar and a drop in blood pressure and heart rate as the body returns to normal.

Short bursts of adrenaline are not harmful but people who enjoy extreme sports sometimes become addicted to the highs it gives, the so-called *adrenaline rush*.

The body doesn't know what the danger is - it just automatically responds to the situation. But *problems* arise when the stress is there *constantly*. For example:

- Unresolved issues with people resulting in anger and bitterness.
- A bad boss or bullying work colleague who create a hostile working environment leading to stress and anxiety for their colleagues.
- Horrible neighbours. My mum and dad had 8 years of living next door to the neighbourhood hangout for teenagers.
- Family arguments (hard to escape from).
- Negative thinking.

Slowly, over the course of the day, such problems will cause adrenaline to enter your bloodstream, the drip-drip effect making you agitated, on edge and struggling to sleep.

Chronic levels of stress cause the body to produce higher and more prolonged levels of the hormone cortisol which, if not checked, can damage the body in much the same way that acid attacks metal! Common side effects are impaired cognitive performance, thyroid problems, high blood pressure, lowered immune function to name but a few!

Your immune system constantly patrols your body looking for rogue cells, which can become cancerous if left unchecked. When you get involved in an adrenalin rush your body stops this and looks for signs of wounds to the skin in order to do a repair. You are affecting your chances of cancer getting stopped in its tracks.

Adrenaline is also released when things get heated in an argument and it can stay active in your body for up to 4 hours. Just fresh from one yesterday I can confirm I felt exhausted for hours afterwards. (Teenagers eh!)

All these emotions – rage, unforgiveness, depression, anger, worry, frustration, fear, grief and guilt - can become toxic emotions.

This information puts some *responsibility* and *control* into our hands.

Research shows that people *don't* want to live in an environment where there is:

- Arguing
- Abuse
- Aggression
- Hostility
- Too tight a schedule
- More commitments than we can comfortably handle
- Obligations and responsibilities over which *we have no control.*

Q. So how can we help ourselves?

A. By letting go of anger *quickly* before it turns into bitterness or unforgiveness. This is the best prescription a doctor can give you.

> Cheerful disposition is good for your health; Gloom and doom leaves you bone tired.

Proverbs 17 v22 (The Message)

 The *art of forgiveness* is one of the tools and techniques that will heal you.

Admit how you feel and your part in the matter.

Recognise that you need to get rid of these toxic emotions for your own good.

Trust that God has your best interests at heart.

143

Yes, it is difficult but *you will* begin to benefit!

Just look at the tree now.
The roots of *taking charge, forgiveness and communication* will produce the fruit that makes your life sing. You will have the abundant life that Jesus promised in the Bible.

My purpose is to give life in all its fullness.

(John 10:10 Living Bible)

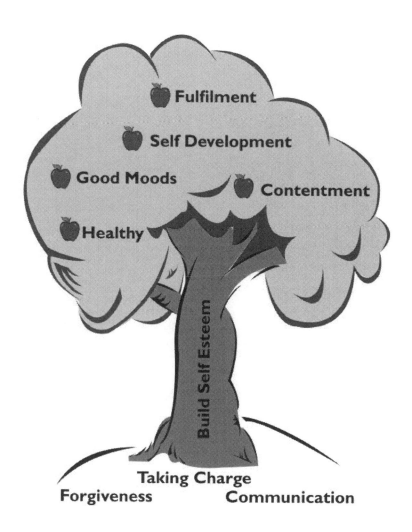

I have practised **the *art of forgiveness*** over the years and I have felt all the benefits in that tree. It's not easy but we can all make a change.

In my 20s, I loved smoking but *I knew it was bad for me* and we now know that the secondary smoke is *bad for those around us.* With God's help I gave up. (It was really easy as they started to taste vile!) My physical health *improved* immediately and I was nicer to be around because I didn't *stink* of smoke.

Living in an atmosphere of peace, joy and encouragement feels great!

Practising the ***art of forgiveness*** means:

- **Learning to apologise quickly.** We all make mistakes so recognising and admitting your faults is a great pain saver.

- **Asking for forgiveness from your friends.** If you *know* that you've upset someone, practise humility and go patch it up. They are often as glad as you to be at peace again.

- **If you are a Christian, confessing your sins to God.** The knowledge that you are *unconditionally* forgiven for everything brings power to your armory and is morally and spiritually uplifting.

- **Forgiving yourself!** Don't listen to your own negative self-talk. Knock those parrots of guilt and shame off your shoulders.

For Christian brothers and sisters

Don't listen to the enemy; he wants you to think that God is mad at you - no way!
Jesus died for *all* your sins before you were even born. He knows what you're going to do in the future, *good and bad.*
Nothing about you comes as a surprise to Him.

Accepting that your behaviour has not produced good choices, is the key to getting back on track.

I once made a decision that could have affected someone else very badly. I felt awful for days and in the midst of it, I heard the devil say, 'You've done it now.' At church, I sat on some chewing gum and there was the devil again telling me that the badness was going to stick to me. In circumstances like this, *knowing God's word* can release you from the tight grip of fear. I turned to this verse for comfort:

God is faithful; He will not let you be tempted beyond what you can bear. But when you are tempted, he will also provide a way out so that you can endure it.

(1 Corinthians 10:13 New International Version)

God always provides a way out by giving us the power to overcome our difficulties and, in a miraculous way, He created an opportunity for me to put things right before it was too late. I still had to honour my original decision, which took courage, but I knew I had made the right choice. I felt such *joy* the moment I sorted it and the outcome wasn't bad. It turned on its head and I got a blessing out of it. *God is good.*

Don't automatically blame other people

When something goes wrong, it triggers a deep need within us to explain what caused the problem. And the easiest way of finding the cause is to *blame someone else*! Unfortunately, this can make us quick to judge others and equally quick to avoid or deny responsibility.

So, be honest with yourself. Have you contributed to the problem? Holding a grudge is like keeping an account on deposit. It's likely that you will make a withdrawal sometime, like a volcano erupting.

Neuroscientists have discovered that we have the ability to override thoughts that lead to actions. For example, feeling hungry prompts us to go prepare some food but, for a time, this basic need can be overridden by an even stronger desire to fast.

The Bible is unified by a number of major themes and one of the most important (and challenging!) is *forgiveness*. When we feel hurt and deeply wounded, we don't want to forgive the person responsible because it feels as if we are allowing them to get away with it. Letting go of negative emotions is the key to our good health and we find in the Bible that God will give us the strength to forgive:

I can do all things through Christ who strengthens me.

(Philippians 4:13 New King James Version)

God commands us to forgive others and enables us to accomplish it.

Lewis B. Smedes (Christian author and theologian) put it this way:

To forgive is to set a prisoner free and discover that the prisoner was you.

God tells us to *have faith* in what He says and that:

In all things God works for the good of those who love him, who have been called according to his purpose.

(Romans 8:28 New International Version)

We are *'called according to his purpose'* to bring about what is good and right. Don't regard forgiveness *solely* as an undeserved kindness that we extend to those who have hurt us. It is also a gift we give ourselves that brings considerable physical and psychological benefits. If you are starting the process of forgiveness, this Bible verse will encourage you:

Don't repay evil for evil. Wait for the Lord to handle the matter.

(Proverbs 20:22 Living Bible)

I trust that my God will make it up to me. He will put things right in His way. We often want to see someone get their comeuppance, and sometimes we do, but that's not God's way.

 I nearly got myself in trouble when I wanted to take things into my own hands. A builder wasn't doing a job to the standard that we expected for the price quoted so before he could completely mess it up, Tony sacked him. I was furious at the lies he had told in order to get the job – he had misled us and ripped us off. I secretly plotted to send him dog dirt in the post - terrible, I know! I planned how I would go about it and I even thought of driving to Cumbria to post it so he wouldn't work out it was me! Fortunately, my Bible readings at the time contained the verse quoted above and that brought me to my senses before I did something foolish that I would later regret.

You have to answer these questions in the light of what I've shared.

Q. Am I willing to carry this around for the rest of the year or even my life *knowing* it is affecting my mental and physical health and wellbeing? Who is suffering? Am I drinking the poison?

Forgiveness is a choice

The highest summit of self-control is praying for those who don't deserve it.
(The homilies of St John Chrysostom)

It takes guts and maturity. A major *attitude change* is required to overcome the hardness that creeps into

149

your heart and mind - like a cancer, it will eat away at you. When we forgive, we free ourselves of anger, resentment and bitterness all of which prevent us from living in the present moment where the good things in life happen.

The benefits of forgiveness are worth striving for. We are less angry and anxious; we sleep soundly and relate well to other people. Our general attitude is more positive, optimistic and joyful. All this contributes to our emotional and physical wellbeing. That *strike to your heart* when you see someone who has hurt or annoyed you, will disappear.

Try this exercise to see how many people you are actually holding a grudge against.

 Sit comfortably in a chair and close your eyes. Now imagine yourself seated in your chair in the centre of a room. In front of you is a green door, the handle is turning and in comes someone you've chosen from your friends or family.

Q. As you see them entering, what is your *gut feeling* towards that person?

Q. Did your heart sink or sing? Make a mental note.

Q. Who were you pleased to see?

Q. Who did you groan at as they walked into the room?

Keep doing this for everyone you come into contact with regularly. You will be very surprised at the ones towards whom you have feelings of distaste or hostility.

When I did this exercise, I was shocked at the feelings I had hidden away. *Lots of niggles I hadn't expected.*

These feelings were subconsciously affecting my inner peace.

150

I took steps, *some of them painful*, to put things right.

- For some, it meant a kind word I hadn't said for ages.
- For others, it was letters of apology.
- A smile at someone I'd been avoiding.

It didn't happen overnight but as opportunities arose, I took them.

I felt so clean and light as I worked towards righting my wrongs.

 There was a situation in the 1990s, which made me feel sick whenever I thought of it. It was very difficult because the people involved were attending the same church. Every week the service was spoilt for me because there was always a conflict raging in my mind about how best to avoid them without revealing my feelings. One day I was talking to God about this in the car, screaming at Him to release me from this sickness and burden that was affecting me so badly each Sunday. I hadn't begun to research the information I'm sharing with you now so this anguish went on for 3 years! With Gods help it was successfully resolved shortly after that but what a dreadful waste of those years for everyone concerned.

However in later years, I had studied enough to enable me to apply it to my own situation. When I met my husband Tony in 1978, he owned a motorbike. He soon had what every girlfriend dreads, an accident. It was a very bizarre experience because I actually had a premonition about it and, to his astonishment, I beat him to the Accident and Emergency Department. Thankfully, he wasn't badly injured but I told him if he got another motorbike, he'd be looking for a new girlfriend! (Sounds tough but I hadn't quite fallen in love with him yet!) I was pleased that he cared enough for me to promise that he would *never ever* get another one.

Roll forward 25 years and Tony started to have thoughts of recapturing his youth. Despite protests from me, his son James and both our mothers, he went

151

ahead and ordered a Harley Davidson. I told him how upset I was that he was going back on his promise. He wouldn't listen when I told him that many men of his age were being killed in road accidents because traffic conditions had changed so much since he was a teenager.

Gradually, over the weeks, I could feel resentment creeping into our marriage. I began to see his decision to get a bike as a sign that his love for me had diminished. After all, why would someone go against a heartfelt plea? My attitude towards him grew cold and I stopped talking to him – he didn't even notice! I began to get depressed as I realised that he cared more about getting a bike than he did for my feelings. I wrote him a letter but he only read the first 3 lines before dismissing it as piffle and telling me to get over it. Anger then ensued and I began to despise him. When the bike finally arrived, I refused to even sit on it, never mind go for a ride with him. I couldn't bring myself to share his excitement and delight – I was turning into a real pain!

Four months down the line, I was researching forgiveness in preparation for Confidence Gym and immediately I realised that I had become a victim of all the things I've mentioned earlier in this session. Now I was armed with something to help me save my ailing marriage. This is how I managed to rescue my relationship even though Tony had caused me so much pain and anguish.

I *chose* to forgive him.

The choice is straightforward. Either you do or you don't.

Remember that *it's you* who benefits.

 It's a process and, just like a complicated instruction manual, it can take time to work through. But there is a *quick start guide* you can access immediately to get started. This is how to do it.

Say, 'I forgive them.' *Force* it out loud - then repeat it.

Like most changes, it's getting started that's the hardest part. **Don't just think it, *say it, force it* out of your mouth** (through gritted teeth if necessary!) **and then keep *repeating it*.** You are giving an instruction to your subconscious mind that will be acted upon, creating feelings in line with your will for peace of mind.

I followed this process in my bike dilemma, repeating it several times a day and then I added some positive words:

Buying this bike doesn't mean he no longer loves me.

I will feel better when I've forgiven him.

I forgive him and I am going to feel better.

I had a young son to think about and I didn't want him to grow up with parents who couldn't talk to each other or even ended up getting divorced. My experience may pale into insignificance when compared with what you are going through at the moment but the truth is, *we all make mistakes.*

Others may overlook what *you* have done one day, even if you don't deserve it. I'm so glad that we have the capacity within us to free ourselves from the consequences of other people's bad decisions or selfish desires.

 It can be helpful to have a good friend to help you get started or to *be accountable to* for your progress. In this, I've been blessed with my friend Amy, 24 years my junior. She pointed out the urgency for me to forgive and then committed the whole thing to prayer and fasting. I was astonished that someone else would do that for me! I had never fasted before but Amy's selflessness prompted me to give it my best shot, along with daily pronouncements of forgiveness as I got on with my housework. Two weeks later when she asked me how I felt, I said, 'Better but not 100% yet.' But I was feeling more relaxed and less angry as my subconscious mind began to obey the order to forgive. Two weeks later when I saw Amy

again, I was able to confidently say that I felt terrific! I was so grateful for her support and that she'd had the courage to challenge me in the first place. Incidentally he decided to sell his bike 2 years later. Hot off the press April 2016. He's just asked me if he can buy another bike. I've said yes. He wants to go this afternoon in case I change my mind!

You may not be in the right place to forgive just now and I understand that but please think about your mental and physical health and wellbeing. It's worth giving forgiveness a try. *All these benefits are within your reach.*

God has designed you with the ability and the power to change your mind. The Bible says:

Fix your attention on God. You'll be changed from the inside out.

(Romans 12:2 The Message)

Forgiveness can open doors that have remained locked for years. It is the weapon of choice when it comes to repairing relationships. Being a 5%er in this area will bring you dividends of untold joy and peace.

Over to you!

The next chapter on Happiness will explain more fantastic reasons to keep good emotions at the forefront of your mind.

- Stress kills Confidence.

- Have a good life balance, keep your tank full.

- You've got to work with what you've got.

- Sharing is helpful.

- Our confidence is robbed when we don't feel in control

- Lots of stress is self - generated.

- Give family members a higher tolerance level.

- Do we need new glasses?

- Worry produces stress.

- Use Socratic questioning to resolve your worries.

- Disease can be caused by dis-ease.

- Let go of anger quickly.

- Practice the ART of Forgiveness.

3

How to
Increase
Happiness

This is what everyone really wants to know.

I was in Boots, the chemist, around the time I was researching this session and I noticed a series of 5 booklets entitled *Change One Thing*. They were free from the pharmacy section and covered such subjects as *How to Lose Weight* and *How to Stop Smoking*. But the one that really caught my attention was *How to Feel Happier*. Unfortunately, it was out of stock but all the other titles were piled high. I tried for weeks to get it and eventually after going to the shop 3 times in one week, I managed to get my precious booklet. When I asked the assistant why it was so hard to come by she said that as soon as they got a delivery, they just flew off the shelf. The information in the booklet was no more than a sales promotion to make you buy products but it did get me thinking about the whole subject and it prompted me to start doing my own research. These are my findings.

Where does happiness come from?

Why are some folks so grumpy and others bubbly?

Research shows that **50%** of our natural happiness setting comes from our upbringing, our DNA and our *learned* behaviours. So yes parents, it does matter how *we* behave.

We all have a *set* point of happiness which is related to the first 5 years of our lives. Some research was done in the USA with lottery winners who were observed from 1978 onwards. The findings were that although the money had brought them happiness for a short time, they eventually returned to the happiness level they had been at before winning.

Doctors' surgeries are full of people taking 40 years to get over the first 5 and *some never do so.*

Research conducted by a neurobiologist at Harvard University Medical School has concluded that hugs are as vital to the health and development of children as food and water. A lack of touching and attention stunts their growth and adversely affects their behaviour. In adult life they are less likely to be happy and emotionally well balanced.

A lovely lady I know told me she feels very unhappy because her daughter never hugs her. This really shouldn't come as any surprise to her though because she admitted that she didn't hug her daughter when she was a child. She said she was too busy!

Part of the Harvard study included experiments with children in Romanian orphanages. Many of us will remember the TV reports in the 1980s showing them rocking to and fro in cots, starved of love and attention. People were appalled at the sight of these young children crowded into dreary, meagerly staffed orphanages, without hugs, toys or activities.

To determine how hugs and other forms of physical contact might change a child's life, 30 of the orphans participated in an enrichment programme for 13 months. A carer was assigned to every 4 children instead of 20 as was usual. The carer played with the children, showed them toys, picked them up and cuddled them. The enrichment helped the children enormously but when the programme ended and they returned to their original conditions that involved little touching, the physical and behavioural advantage they had obtained faded. Once again, they became socially withdrawn and unable to respond normally to other children and adults.

If your children have already grown up there's still your *grandchildren* who can benefit and actually a hug at any age is therapeutic. Later, I'll tell you how I believe that a regular hug healed a relative.

10% of happiness comes from our *environment*. Where we live, pleasant streets, good neighbours and our material possessions. When I moved from a large new town development to a small village and a detached house with double garage, longed for en-suite and open fire, I was really happy! I'm pleased to say that this happiness increase has stayed with me too. Before that I was always wishing that I just had this

159

and that but I'm a simple girl at heart and once I'd got what I wanted, I appreciated it every day. More about that later.

The remaining **40%** of happiness comes from our *attitude and outlook.*

This is great news because it means *we are in control* of a significant percentage of our happiness level. Our attitude and outlook means not letting anyone steal our joy or depending on someone or something else to make us feel happy.

Happiness is a skill that can be learned.

Please read that good news again and let it sink in.

Everything we experience is recorded as information in our brains. If we are able to control it, we can decide what our lives will be like.

Life is 10 per cent what happens to us and 90 percent how we handle it.

 We have 2 cats that get up to all kinds of mischief. One evening when we were watching TV, a mouse ran from one chair to the other. It gave us such a shock. Our male cat, who had brought it into the house to play with, was nowhere to be seen and our other cat was too timid to confront it and just sat watching where it had run to. I told Tony to get something to catch it with but he promptly jumped up on the settee freaking out! Laughing, I calmly ran to the kitchen for a large glass bowl and after lifting the couch to make the mouse run into a corner, I plopped the bowl on top of it. I told it how lucky it had been and placed it outside in the garden. It amused Tony how differently we had reacted to the same problem.

It's not the problem but your response to it **that changes each situation into a good one.** *You are in control of your thinking.*

We need to look at life in a different way. We all know that true happiness isn't found in more money,

160

possessions, influence, makeup, shoes and holidays etc but in life's simple pleasures; talking with friends; taking a walk in the countryside; reading a good book; cooking your favourite meal and strengthening family ties. I think we are finally realising this. Seven years after writing my original notes, I have seen more and more websites and magazines aimed at simplifying our lives.

Happiness is within reach of us all

Ponder this quote from Roy M Goodman, an American politician:

Happiness is a way of travel, not a destination.

We often strive to attain what we think will bring us joy only to find when we get it, that something else has popped into our thoughts and off we go again on the treadmill. Are you trying to convince yourself that life will be better after you've completed this or that project? Happiness is now, where you are in this moment, doing what you are doing without worrying about the outcome. The truth is *there's no better time to be happy than right now*. If not now, when? Your life will always be filled with challenges and changes.

 *The secret is to be happy where you are.*

In the Bible, Paul the Apostle said that he could be content whatever the circumstances:

I've learned by now to be quite content whatever my circumstances. I'm just as happy with little as with much, with much as with little. I've found the recipe for being happy whether full or hungry, hands full or hands empty.
(Philippians 4:12 The Message)

We need to *live in the now*, value the choices we make and look for true meaning in our lives. Choosing to live in the past or the future not only robs you of enjoyment today, it robs you of living life to the full. You can only live one moment at a time so you might as well make it the present!

All this takes an investment of time - looking at your life and making some changes to those stale routines we talked about.

Why strive for happiness?

Some of you are thinking, 'Why bother? I'm all right as I am.'

Because it keeps us going - we live longer!

Here's the science. We produce *50% more antibodies* when we are in a happy frame of mind. Later on, I'll be sharing how having a laugh benefits our wellbeing with some verses from the Bible to back it up.

There's no 'one size fits all' solution. Each of us must raise *our* bar and not compare ourselves with anyone else.

An exciting find whilst studying for this session was a BBC2 TV programme called *Making Slough Happy.* (I bought the book and the reference is in the index for those of you who really want to make big changes). This was a social experiment conducted over a 3-month period on a group of Slough volunteers to try and improve their happiness levels. The philosophy of happiness was condensed into simple actions such as counting your blessings; phoning a friend you've lost touch with; taking regular physical exercise; doing a good turn every day; having a laugh etc.

They found that the most important path to happiness is in *our relationships* **with individuals and communities**, even random people on the street or in the supermarket. Importantly, they found that you can't enhance your wellbeing by having more material possessions. At the start, the volunteers' happiness rating was 6 out of 10 but by the end, there was a 33% upward shift to 8 out of 10. They experienced an *increased level of happiness* particularly in relationships and work.

So clearly, it is possible to reprogramme our happiness setting.

So what steps can we take to become happier?

 Firstly, we must *change old attitudes*. Where have we heard that before?

1. Look for the good in everything

This is very powerful when you learn to put it into practice as a *habit*.

 As I approached my 50th birthday I found that I needed to counteract the negative feelings about growing old that were buzzing round in my head. So I looked for benefits such as cheaper car insurance. There is a company for the over 50s that offers a 25% discount because this age group doesn't have as many accidents so now at aged 56, my insurance is peanuts – yippee!

I was sharing this principle with a friend. I was telling her about my son James who had a surprise infestation of head lice which unfortunately had also transferred to Tony and I. She challenged me to find something good to say about it! Not to be beaten, I gave it some thought and came up with some pretty surprising things. Firstly, we had to comb out a million eggs that had been laid on our heads. You can't accomplish this on your own so we would spend an hour together each evening head-combing, chatting about the day's events and telling jokes. James and I had a great time looking through the magnifying glass as we picked them out to examine in detail for a little science lesson. We had to be fully focussed on the task in hand so the TV and all other distractions were switched off. Crazy though it may sound, this was real quality family time! Secondly, I was worried that these critters might be hiding in our pillows so I swapped ours for the new ones in the guest bedroom. And guess what, they were way more comfy than ours! Don't worry if you ever stay at my house, I found out that they die if they don't feed for 24 hours.

When James broke his ankle, looking for a positive slant helped me to get through a difficult and tiresome time. There were benefits for both of us. James had me waiting on him like a little lord. He was off school so I didn't have to do the school run or make up his packed lunch every day. He couldn't go to his drama class which saved me a drive and £40 in tuition fees. He was able to game all day without me nagging him to tidy his room.

It just needs a thought adjustment for you to feel better about the situation. This technique is called *reframing - same picture but looks different*.

You're controlling how it affects you.

A while ago my dentist retired. After 2 years the new dentist noticed that I was having 4 hygienist visits per year instead of two like everyone else. I explained that my old dentist had allowed me to have the 2 extra appointments because I liked the clean feeling it gave me. She explained that there was no medical need for this and so I would have to pay for these extra treatments if I wanted to continue with them. No thanks I thought, that would be an extra bill of £88. I went home really cross at my dental reduction. It bothered me for days until I began to put into practice my teaching. I suddenly thought 'Y'know what, I've actually had 2 years free treatment, brilliant! I immediately felt better about the whole matter. This comment I heard on TV sums up reframing perfectly:

The happiest people are not those who have the best of everything. No, the happiest people are those who make the best of everything.

2. Trust in God

When I was 17 I started work in the food department of a large store. I did really well and the Staff Manageress promised me the window dresser's job which was soon to become vacant. It was the best gig to get because you worked on your own initiative with no direct boss, you could display your style for all to see and you also wore a really smart outfit. It inspired me to work even harder but then disaster struck - she left to go and live in London.

The new Staff Manageress didn't feel the same way about me and one night going home on the bus my friend, who was the senior window dresser, told me that another girl in the food department was going to get the job – apparently it was because she was no good when it came to serving customers and they needed to get her out of the way. And in my view, she was lazy too! I was stunned and sobbed my heart out. How cruel that someone who didn't deserve that great job had got it by default. I felt robbed and cried all evening. I was so upset I couldn't even control my breathing, and mum couldn't tell what I was saying for 10 minutes. Mum suggested I should look for another job but I didn't take her advice and unfortunately over the next few weeks, my love of the job just died and I wasn't putting in the same effort and enthusiasm as before.

One morning I received a written warning from the new Staff Manageress because I had given a regular customer's disabled daughter a piece of cheese that we were going to scrap. This was the final straw and that afternoon I went to the Job Centre. That's when I found an amazing job that was to change the course of my life, and that of my husband to be, forever. The strange thing was, it had been up for a few weeks and they just hadn't found the right person. My career in newspaper advertising was about to start.

Looking back, I know that I was never meant to stay in retailing. My talents lay in sales, presentations, competition, targets, customer service and staff training. Had I got the window dressing job I wouldn't be the person I am now because the training I received in newspaper advertising was first class - it gave me life skills that I still use today. At the time it seemed as if my whole world had collapsed and perhaps some of you have had similar experiences. But fear not because God has everything worked out and is in control even for those of us (like me!) who are stubborn and need a push before they will make a change. Don't let an unfortunate circumstance *force* you to act, just do it! Go with the flow.

Very often we *think* we have got things worked out just *fine*. We *fail* to see how life can be much better and instead, we *settle* for mediocrity.

 Once upon a time, a duckling found its way into our garden. Not a good idea as we have 2 cats! We caught it quickly and took it to our neighbour who had a small duck pond. But Marmaduke, as we christened him, kept returning again and again narrowly escaping being eaten by our cats. It was hard work catching him but the danger he was putting himself in made us act quickly each time to secure his safety. But one day, we just couldn't catch him because he knew all the places to hide. The next day I was sick with worry because I knew he was still somewhere in the garden. Just as I was pondering what to do, he popped up on the patio and that gave me an idea. I got a slice of bread, opened the patio door slightly and began throwing crumbs in his direction enticing him nearer and nearer until finally, I grabbed him! Triumphantly, I took him upstairs and ran him a bath and he swam around quite contentedly for 3 hours until Tony came home. But Marmaduke couldn't stay in the bath forever so we decided to take him to my mum's in Darwen. There is a large duck pond opposite her house and she had told me that local boys had smashed many of this year's eggs and the mummy ducks were swimming around forlornly. We popped Marmaduke into our cat basket and drove over to Darwen. As soon as we let him out at the edge of the pond, a female duck flew over to look after him, taking him across the pond to meet the others. I cried when I realised that this is exactly how God is with us. We get into trouble, we want to do our own thing and we often fight against what He might be trying to do in our lives, like Marmaduke hiding in our garden. All we wanted to do was set him in a place of safety where he could flourish – just as God does with us. When I look back, I can see God's hand in everything that's happened to me, good and

4

bad, and if I continue to trust in Him, I know He will look after me and my interests.

Have you ever seen the BBC TV programme *Hustle*? It's about 5 confidence tricksters who go after baddies who have robbed people. It shows how the team use elaborate schemes, trickery and double-crossing to take cash from the unsuspecting victim or *mark* as they are called. Meticulous planning and ingenuity prevail to force the baddies to make up for their wrongs. However, at the end of the programme something always goes wrong and it looks as if they've failed in their task. But 'hey ho', just when you think all is lost, you are shown lots of little things that have been *going on behind the scenes* and which make everything turn out exactly as planned.

That's just what God is doing with us. We have no idea what He's up to but you can be sure it's always for our benefit. We just need to trust Him and have faith. Interestingly, the day after my window dressing job bombshell, I went to the pub with a friend and met my husband to be, Tony. Even when everything seems hopeless, God throws in something good to distract us!

3. Don't miss the miracles

In 2003 my great aunt's husband died unexpectedly. She was in her 90s but he was 23 years younger and was expected to outlive her. She lived 18 miles away in Blackpool. It fell upon me to provide care along with her nephew and I would visit her every Friday.

Two years after his death, she received a letter from an insurance company saying that they were looking into a claim her late husband had submitted shortly before his death. My aunt had tripped over an uneven flag in the street and hurt herself quite badly. They wanted to interview her to ask questions about her state of health at the time, the effect of the fall and also to compare her present state of health. At 93, my aunt's memory wasn't at its best so I said I would go along to the interview to help her with the questions. During the interview, something struck me for the first time. Yes, my aunt's health had been affected. The pain of osteoporosis made it difficult for her to sleep and she needed regular injections for her back. She was also having panic attacks that affected her heart so she had to carry an emergency nitro lingual spray in her pocket at all times. What I realised though was that *all* these symptoms had *disappeared* and she was completely well.

A miracle had happened under our noses and we had missed it!

It's good to look back and see how far you've come along. My aunt had been in poor health for 10 years and at her advanced age, it would have been unrealistic to expect any change for the better. But since I had been looking after her and visiting regularly, there was a marked improvement. I put this down to lots of *hugs* and attention during my weekly visits. We would sit cuddled up next to each other as she told me old family stories which I really enjoyed listening to.

So take time to see what changes have been taking place in your life and you may be very surprised. You can then give thanks for these things which help to build up your contentment levels.

4. Appreciate what you've got

Here's a challenge for you. Right now, get a pen and write down in 2 minutes all the things you are thankful for. Don't read on until you have done this.

Unless you have done this exercise you won't realise how *unappreciative* you really are. When we do this at Confidence Gym, we have an average of 15 items but a lady who got 62 things in 2 minutes holds the record!

What she had done was to break down the different components of her life. She was appreciating in detail, people and possessions. For example, did your list include a warm bed to sleep in; food on your table; a roof over your head; clean drinking water on tap; good health etc? Most people's lists don't include these basic things which we tend to take for granted.

 **Q.** What would you give up if you were made to choose between your eyesight and your hearing?

At this point, everyone in the room is wearing a blindfold to experience life without sight. Each person tries to identify everyday objects but only around half ever manage to do so correctly. It really brings home the challenge of being without a vital sense.

To experience this for yourself, I encourage you to close your eyes and try to make your way out of the room you are in without looking. (But do check first that you're not going to trip over something!). Or just try peeling potatoes, *not* cutting them!

Remember my **5%er** talk. If you don't do these exercises you won't fully understand and learn the principle. It's great fun especially if you get other family members to join in.

I've read many articles about cancer sufferers appreciating life much more – they become aware of the real richness that surrounds them every day. For some, that day may be their last. The same goes for near death survivors. After a brush with death, they have a heightened appreciation of the gift of life. Wouldn't it be wonderful to appreciate these things without having to experience pain and trauma first?

You can, and it will warm the cockles of your heart I promise!

This is a great habit to build into your life every day or, at the very least, once a week. Every evening before you go to sleep, have a time of thankfulness for the day's basic things that you have been blessed with.

I like this story that illustrates the point so well. A family of 12 are constantly falling out about living together. The husband and wife consult a counsellor for guidance on how to best manage the situation. To their surprise, he tells them to move a goat into the house to live with them for a week. In desperation, they follow the advice but it's a pretty grim time with the goat pooing, chewing everything and bleating constantly. At their next consultation, the counsellor tells them to get rid of the goat and see him again in a week's time. They are so relieved and a week later they return relaxed and happy. Being without the goat taught them to appreciate life!

Every day, we take things for granted. You will find that taking stock of what you have is a really energising tonic - no gin required!

5. Concentrate on what went right

In 2002 we went on holiday to St Ives and stayed in a beautiful flat with panoramic views overlooking the beach. But it takes so long to get to Cornwall – at least 8 hours from Lancashire. So we set off at 6 am and found to our surprise that there were very few cars on the road and no traffic jams. By mistake we undershot an exit at Exeter on the M5 only to find an empty café where we were served with scrumptious food in only 5 minutes! As we rejoined the motorway, we could see long queues at the services where we usually stop so our earlier mistake turned out to be a real blessing. We drove down in 6 hours 45 minutes which was an all time record. As we approached our destination, the sun came out to give us a warm welcome. Our holiday let was beautifully clean and as we looked out towards the horizon, there was a rainbow. Horses were cantering across the beach and seals began flipping up out of the water as if to say, 'The magic begins now.' It was idyllic.

We decided to spend an hour on the beach before dinner but as I stepped onto the sand, it burnt my feet! I began hopping around trying to find a cold spot and shouting for Tony to throw me a towel. Disaster! We hadn't thought to bring one with us. Suddenly, my good mood completely evaporated and I started blaming Tony for everything. In the midst of my tantrum, Tony said, 'STOP! I just can't believe you Susan. We've had a trouble-free journey, good food served in 5 minutes, a sunny magical welcome and you've spoilt it all just because we haven't brought a towel to the beach. Think about all the good things today and don't let one silly little thing spoil it.' Well, that told me! But his words instantly took the heat out of the situation and, of course, he was quite right. I apologised for being such a grump and then I asked him to run up to the flat for a towel!

Too often we go with the negatives and ignore the positives. Focussing on the good rather than the bad is the best policy and can instantly change the situation.

6. Don't compare

I usually illustrate this point with a little play but sharing that on paper won't have the same impact so I'll tell you 2 stories instead.

When I was in my mid-twenties, I was thrilled when my cousin asked me to be her bridesmaid. I was 7 years old the last time I'd been one.

My cousin and I were very close, like sisters. She was the only bridesmaid at my wedding so I was really looking forward to performing the honour for her. On the big day when we were getting ready, I suddenly noticed that one of the other girls had a slightly different dress and a bigger bouquet. I asked another girl why that was and she said, 'Oh Pamela is the maid of honour.' Suddenly I was enraged. How come *she* gets to do that I thought? She's only her friend and I'm her cousin! *It should be me!* I felt really snubbed and to make matters worse, Pamela and I had never got along that well. Instead of proudly walking down the aisle supporting my cousin, I was petulant and resentful. I let it spoil my day.

Before I illustrate the point, I'll tell you about a more recent upset. Around 2006, I had been in church ministry for about 7 years and decided it was time to move on because I wanted to develop Confidence Gym. I was quite excited because other people leaving ministry had always been presented with a massive, very expensive bunch of flowers. On my last day, in anticipation, I got my best large vase out of the cupboard. Kind and complimentary words were said and then I was presented with a £4.99 bunch of flowers from the local supermarket. *What?* Others who had served far fewer years had received enormous gifts. I had to put on a good act of being thrilled but inside, I was seething with indignation because I felt that the gift didn't in any way reflect all my effort and hard work over the years. I left that day really upset.

In both cases, by making comparisons, I had robbed myself of a privilege that was intended for my enjoyment.

This attitude can continue to destroy moments in your life for years. I am thankful that the Lord brought this to my attention just at the time I was putting Confidence Gym together because it taught me a valuable lesson and it also gave me a great teaching opportunity. I apologised to Him for my attitude over the flowers and guess what happened. The next day, quite unexpectedly, I received a huge bunch of flowers from the Head Mistress at James' school as a thank you for all the work I had done with ACT the children's acting club! I was absolutely thrilled but this time, it was less to do with the size of the bunch of flowers and more with the thought and kindness behind the gift. It really is the thought that matters! I gave the small bunch to a good friend who was feeling under the weather and she was thrilled to bits to receive the very same bunch.

I no longer make comparisons and nor do I get jealous of others. I savour what I receive because if you really have been unfairly treated, *you can be sure that God will put it right.*

7. Develop a strategy for coping with stress

I have covered this at length in Session 3 so you can read that if you haven't done so already. But here are some other thoughts.

Stress is always going to be in our lives and reassuringly, research shows that our lives would be less fulfilling if it were not there.

We need to consider what kind of stress it is. Some people work best under time pressure.

Research shows that **90%** of what we worry about will *never* come to pass! So as my aunty Mags said to me once, 'Don't worry about anything unless it happens.'

Another good statement I heard is:

Pessimists may be proved right in the end BUT optimists have a better journey.

There are many other types of stress. It may be a family member who you can't be doing with as they pass through a particular phase of life. In other words, you can't do anything about it so learn to control your responses. Specialist help is always available. Do try prayer first. I always find this makes the most difference.

8. Take control and upgrade your 'to do' list

Feeling that we are in control is a major factor in feeling happy. Setting goals and achieving them makes you *feel* on top of the world.

I believe that we were put on earth to fulfil a purpose and sometimes, when we are not taking steps towards becoming someone who is making a difference, the rotten thoughts of, 'I'm rubbish/useless' can set inside our soul.

Session 2 on *What's my Purpose?* will deliver all the information but for those of you skipping that, I will share this tool I discovered accidently and have been using since my son James was born. After his birth I was constantly tired because he hardly slept for the first 6 months. Tony and I battled to get him to sleep each evening but he was having none of it so we had to manage our own sleep very methodically. I would go to bed at 9pm and Tony had him till about 1pm when I awoke to feed him and see to him during the night. I don't know of any woman who can function on only a few hours sleep – it's bound to take its toll. I found that I couldn't think straight or remember anything, not even which breast he had last fed from and for how long. He hardly drank a thing and was always underweight but praise the Lord, the midwives said he was in perfect health but they still wanted me to keep a record of his feeds.

I got a tiny notebook and began recording the information. Very often as I was feeding James, I would think of things that needed doing and jot them down at the back of the book. As each task was completed, I marked it with a highlighter pen to remind me that I had done it. It was very useful because having everything in one place meant that I could easily track stuff and plan jobs. There was no need to start a new list each day - I just kept the old one rolling on. My confidence and efficiency grew as I could see all the completed tasks and I began to write simple tasks in there too just to give me a buzz of achievement as I crossed through them.

I realised that what had started out from my feelings of desperation, had become the making of me. I introduced this tool at my Confidence Gym sessions and I've had amazing feedback from women who've used it. I even had some blank notebooks specially printed with suggestions of what kind of lists you could make e.g. Christmas shopping lists; books/CDs you've lent out; recording children's temperatures when they're ill; insurances coming due etc. The possibilities are endless! The great thing is that you use it to *suit you*.

The sense of accomplishment has grown my confidence and I've *become happier* as a result of the additional *control* in my life.

Research shows that list makers are the winners in life. Go on, give it a go.

9. Declutter.

This is another way of taking *control*. You can *think* much more clearly when everything around you is well organised. The saying, 'A place for everything and everything in its place' has certainly brought me peace and tranquillity.

There are now many TV programmes about people who have problems getting rid of junk and clutter. Compulsive hoarding is an anxiety disorder and is highly prevalent in the UK where over a million people are thought to be affected. It can interfere with a person's normal day-to-day routine and relationships to such an extent that they are unable to function and have little quality of life. Their clutter is keeping them prisoner both physically and emotionally.

As I write, we are in the process of going through my mum-in-law's flat as she has gone to live in a residential home. We are staggered at what we have found. Whenever we needed anything she would always say she had one but invariably, she couldn't find it and would end up buying another. The outcome of this is that we have found bags and bags of the same products, unused and out of date, all taking up every inch of drawer space, cupboards and the spare bedroom. She couldn't see what she had and this hindered her everyday routine because she just didn't know where to start with it all.

Q. What are you hoarding?

It's not healthy and the whole exercise of going through your stuff and assessing the value of keeping, recycling, giving it to charity or just getting rid, does something on the inside which *frees* you and enables you to *breathe*. I always enjoy seeing the long queues at our local tip after Christmas as people make way for the new and dump the old.

If it feels overwhelming then remember to start **1% by 1%.** Do a room at a time or even a set of drawers. Do one each week and then use the days in between to find a new home for it all. Charity shops will love you and there are always organisations that can find someone else to love your stuff. Car boot sales are great fun and there are many online recycling sites that are worth a look. You have no excuse now as it's all been made so easy. However, some of you may need a little push from someone who has the courage to tell you that at aged 52 you're unlikely to wear that top you bought when you were 16! You may have even friends who will love some of your rubbish so much that they will take it away with them. After all, one man's rubbish is another man's treasure! And think of the money you could make if you sell some of it.

So don't be ashamed of your clutter. Everyone has a dumping spot in the house; it's just that yours is a bit bigger!

Happiness Additives

Here are some more things to add to your Happiness Manifesto:

Food Some foods can make you *feel* happier. Do a bit of research into your favourite foods and find out their nutritional values so that you will feel happier when you eat them. For instance, turkey is high in tryptophan, a feel-good hormone. Blueberries are high in flavonoids which are thought to protect the body's cells from environmental contaminants thereby reducing the risk of heart disease and cancer. Dark chocolate is rich in antioxidants, which are important to cellular health generally, and are key to the functioning of the immune system. Love it or hate it, broccoli contains powerful antioxidants and anticarcinogens which hinder the growth of certain cancers and it also stands out as the most concentrated source of vitamin C. When you take time to investigate what you are putting into your body, you will *become happier* in the knowledge that you are doing your very best to stay healthy.

Remember - you are what you eat!

Exercise. It's probably the last thing you want to hear but exercise is one of the *most effective ways of keeping depression away* quite apart from all the other obvious benefits of having a supple body and encouraging weight loss. Copyright laws prevent me from reproducing a chart I have showing the effect of exercise on depression but I can tell you that there is increasing research evidence which shows that exercise leads to improvements in depression that rival or surpass those from antidepressant drugs. A study conducted by Duke University, North Carolina in the late 1990s divided depressed patients into 3 treatment groups – exercise only; exercise and antidepressant; antidepressant only.

After 6 weeks, the drug-only group was doing slightly better than the other 2 but after 10 months, it was the exercise-only group that had the highest remission and stay-well rate.

The science behind this is too detailed to go into here but the book *Happiness: The Real Medicine and How it Works* by Blair Lewis has more information if you would like to learn more.

So get to it with renewed enthusiasm!

Small treats every day. I thought you would like this one. A little something to look forward to during the day is so uplifting. It can be food, shopping, creative output, anything that you enjoy and look forward to – but not to excess! The emphasis is on *small*. I plan a treat every day and often, it's a new tea flavour I've discovered. But I don't just whiz the kettle on and drink it from a mug while doing a million other things. Instead, I set aside a bit of special me time, drink it from my best china cup and really savour it. You can use your treat as a reward to encourage you to do more with your day but that isn't a real treat. Treat yourself because you're worth it; you really are!

Music. It can produce a number of health benefits including lowering stress levels; raising your state of mind; changing your mood and relaxing or stimulating the brain. It's also useful in meditation or as a preliminary to prayer.

Retailers often use music as a tool to sell things so when you go to the supermarket, the background music isn't for your entertainment – it's to get you to spend more! Low-tempo music makes shoppers move slowly round the store so they end up buying more. The type of music is important too. A wine store found that when they changed from playing pop music to classical, sales increased and customers bought the more expensive wines!

Just sitting down and listening to your favourite music, perhaps something you played on holiday, will take you right back to that happy place and lift your spirits. You can concentrate better, drive better (I've just heard on the radio that one of the safest songs to drive to is *Come Away With Me* by Norah Jones) and perform tasks with a renewed vigour and attitude when good music is on. So make sure you tune into something every day if you can.

Singing is really good for your mood. I'm sure I read somewhere that it's also good for your immune system, but frustratingly I can't remember where I heard it. It really produced an increase in happiness for those participants in the TV programme who joined a choir. Why not make your own music or have a sing-along to the radio or a favourite CD? It doesn't matter if you're not very tuneful. You'll still enjoy it and it will do you the power of good.

Learn a joke or a funny story to tell. Being able to recall something that made you laugh is very powerful and if you aim to get it into a conversation on a daily basis, then it's going to make you cheerful and lively. Others will enjoy it too. I have about 12 stories that pop into my head when I meet new people. I know them so well that they just slip off the tongue quite naturally.

You don't really need to buy a joke book but it does help. I did!

Hugging and touching. In my earlier sessions, I have discussed the power of a hug. There are many books on the subject so check with your local library if you want to know more. But otherwise, just *get hugging*!

I understand that we are all very different and not everyone is comfortable with getting up close and personal. Try *touching* to start with. Just a hand on someone's shoulder; a pat on the back; a squeeze of the hand or a gentle nudge are all effective for you and the recipient. It works with your animals too. There's lots of research about the health benefits of stroking your pet. I suppose *whenever you cultivate love you will get a benefit*. When I hug my big cat (he's a stone in weight) I can't help saying the words, 'I could eat you on a butty!' Of course, I don't actually want to eat him; it's just my way of saying I love him so much that I want more of him. Which leads me nicely into the next additive.

Owning a pet. My cats bring untold joy **each** day as I care for them. The breed I have 'Burmese' are called 'dog cats' because they behave like them in many ways. This is fabulous because we don't have the chore of taking

180

them for a walk each day, although that can be a great way to get out and do more exercise. They follow us all around the garden and are so loving. When I went 15 years without falling pregnant, my current pets at the time were a great comfort to Tony and me. Pets don't have mood swings. They help us live in the now. Physiological tests have shown that stroking and petting animals definitely improves our health. Patients leaving hospitals have recovered quicker when animals have been present in the home setting. Some nursing homes my mum in law has stayed in have let the local cat in for afternoon strokes to witness great joy amongst the residents. They can help us socialise. I remember meeting my second boyfriend Dene as we both met up around the same spot each evening to walk our dogs. They can help in times of bereavement. Feel less nervous and live longer.

Channel wasted time. Oh boy, get this right and you will be leaping with joy! I have this down to a fine art now after having watched the TV programme and read the brilliant book How to be Happy by Liz Hoggard. But first, a word of warning based on my experience of putting this principle into practice. If you apply these suggestions diligently you may find that you sometimes get irritated and impatient because other people, who are not on the same wavelength, unintentionally frustrate your time-saving plans. Stay calm!

Look at all areas of your day and do a bit of a time and motion exercise on *you* – it will pay big dividends.

- **What were you doing in each hour?**
- **Did you waste time and, if so, on what?**
- **Could you have done anything else at the same time?**

When you know that you could do something else whilst you're waiting *it takes the ache out of the wait*. How you apply this will differ from one person to another but, for example, you can check emails and social media whilst you are in the doctor's, the dentist or a hospital appointment, instead of reading the rubbishy celebrity gossip magazines. Or read up on something from the web; take your favourite book; take

181

a note pad and pen to think of a new recipe or write some encouraging notes to folks.

Every time my car goes in for a service, I write letters to people that I've not been able to keep in touch with. You know it's going to involve a wait so by *taking control* you will be less frustrated and you won't keep looking at the clock every 2 minutes!

Stuck in the car at traffic lights or a traffic jam, I make full use of the wait by doing pelvic floor and beauty and laughter exercises. (You would have to be in the seminar to fully appreciate this tip! I may have a link for you to watch so check the website). I also have a cleaning cloth in the car door so I'll clean the dashboard and windows. And there's a bag at the ready to collect any accumulated rubbish. I apply lippy but usually run out of time when the lights change! Keeping occupied stops me moaning and groaning. It makes me feel happier. Try it!

Increase friendships or deepen the ones you already have. Recent research has found that people with lots of friends live longer. Friends are like a second family but this time *we get to choose them*. The pay off comes in to play the older we get. We may lose our life partner and good friends can fill the gap.

> Just as lotions and fragrance give sensual delight, a sweet friendship refreshes the soul.

Proverbs 27 v 9 (The Message)

Discover what you are good at and do more of it. In the psychology of happiness, this is called *flow* – it's when you get completely absorbed with an activity you absolutely love. It gives you a natural high and feelings of deep enjoyment. So take your mind off the mundane for an hour or so and *increase your hobbies,*

Biodanza. This is a self-development system that uses music and dance to deepen self-awareness, reduce stress and enhance your sense of well-being. When I read about it, I immediately knew it was true because unknowingly,

182

I had been practicing it for 10 years when I was in a dance group. If you've attended Session 4 of Confidence Gym you will have physically performed this exercise and probably voted it one of the favourite things you did on the whole course.

Somewhere in the UK there is a small group of women in their 70s that travel around the country taking this wonderful experience to various ladies' gatherings. Any group can do it - it just involves standing in a circle, catching someone's eye and then both of you dancing across the circle past each other. You have to do it in silence and it's hilarious. In my dance group, we used this technique as a warm-up and I found that it built trust and friendship within the group.

Dance movement develops feelings and connectivity, raises energy levels and enables you to express yourself without being judged. You let your barriers down and it just seems to work on a supernatural level. It makes you feel happy!

Laughter & Smiling.
In session 1 I explained the powerful effect a smile had on my neighbour. What I didn't explain was when you smile YOU get a boost of feel good hormones.
As the corners of your lips extend up to your eyebrows a dose of chemicals is released into your system. That's why I smile at myself in the mirror each morning, no matter how I feel. So smile more!

Contemporary scientific evidence on the effectiveness of laughter and its health benefits is overwhelming but long ago, the Bible said that laughter and a happy heart is like good medicine (Proverbs 17:22). Laughter promotes feel-good hormones and improves our feelings of *social connectedness* when we come together and interact with other people.

I was surprised to read recently that on average, a child laughs 300 times a day while we adults can only manage a measly 17! When you watch young children, you see that they find delight and amusement in the most ordinary or silly things so perhaps it's time for us to rediscover our playful inner child!

Let's look at the health benefits for starters. Laughter helps you sleep so try watching a comedy programme before bed. My husband often watches these late at night to relax and his laughter is infectious - I've actually recorded him laughing because it makes me laugh to hear him enjoying himself. I'm sure it's no coincidence that he falls asleep within 30 seconds of his head hitting the pillow!

According to Professor of Psychiatry, William Fry at Stanford University California, laughter is the equivalent of internal jogging. One minute of laughter is equal to 10 minutes on the rowing machine! It increases the blood flow and provides good cardiac, abdominal, facial and back muscle conditioning.   Full-on belly laughs give your diaphragm and abdominals an aerobic workout. It oxygenates the blood allowing for better circulation and gets the lymphatic system going.

In 1979 Norman Cousins wrote *Anatomy of an Illness: As Perceived by the Patient, which* brought the subject of humour therapy to the attention of the medical profession.   He was hospitalised with a rare crippling disease and when it was diagnosed as incurable, he checked out of the hospital. He knew the harmful effects of negative emotions on the body and reasoned that the reverse might be true.   He started watching old Marx Brothers' films and *Candid Camera* reruns and found that 10 minutes of laughter gave him 2 hours of pain-free sleep. Amazingly, his disease was eventually reversed.

Laughter decreases stress chemicals in our bodies, protecting against depression by raising serotonin levels. It also increases endorphins; the morphine-like chemicals that help diminish pain while triggering positive feelings.

Just as stress weakens the immune system, laughter boosts it by increasing immune cells and infection-fighting antibodies thus improving our resistance to illness and disease. Some research was conducted with a group of couples some of whom were getting married (happy) and some, divorced (unhappy). They blistered the backs of their

184

hands and noticed that those getting married healed within 4 days whereas those divorcing took over a week.

At Confidence Gym, after I've given all this amazing information about health benefits, I get the ladies to do some laughter exercises. You see there is a brilliant fact I've not told you yet and it's that **laughter can be faked and your nervous system can't tell the difference!** It thinks the laughter is real so you get all the benefits.

I've tricked my nervous system for many years, not just pretending to laugh but also imagining I'm doing amazing feats of courage or achieving great things like climbing Everest; winning an Oscar; writing a best seller; taking bullets for royalty and saving people trapped in the channel tunnel! Oh yes, it's dangerous work and I've died 17 times but had some heartfelt funerals. The Queen attended 3 of them and of course I've risen from the dead twice, amazing everyone in the church as they mourned. Yes, you can have some fun with it and create the feelings of joy, hope, achievement, elation etc *without* actually doing any of the work! But you've given yourself a mini holiday with plenty of feel-good chemicals flowing through your body bringing health benefits galore. You may think I'm crazy but why not try it before you knock it!

God created us in His own image and the fact that we have a sense of humour and the ability to laugh out loud tells us what our God is like. He also knew that we would need laughter to cope with life's ups and downs. No other species that He created has this *gift* because that's exactly what it is. God also knew that passing wind through our bottoms and mouths as we eat would cause lots of giggles and silly jokes and as *He* designed us, He did it on purpose. What an awesome God he is.

Research shows that loving and serving others is at the top when it comes to happiness.

If you are a Christian, this will be no surprise to you as it is one of the main teachings of the Bible. Jesus came to serve others and left us an example that has changed the world we live in today. Throughout its long history the Christian Church has been a major source of social services like education and medicine, has inspired our culture and philosophy and has been politically influential. The local church operates in the heart of the community bringing help and hope where none seems possible. The research shows that religious/spiritual people are happier on the whole and tend to live longer. They also recover more quickly from operations.

Mother Theresa lived a simple life but she touched others including those who didn't benefit directly from her care. She inspired so many people to follow in her footsteps. Seeing good things happen to others produces a feel-good effect called *elevation.* Good eh?

Belonging to your local church where you are in a position to help others less fortunate than yourself, will bring great joy and fulfilment to your life. I know this because I do it all the time with many others who have discovered that *it is better to give than receive.* In Third World countries where people live in poverty, research has shown that those who help each other in order to survive often have a much greater sense of community and belonging than in wealthy western nations where feelings of isolation and depression are on the increase. In collective societies, the social emphasis is on the importance of the group's interests rather than those of the individual.

Volunteering is our last additive. It will always bring a purpose to your life, which in turn, will increase your happiness. Organise some events with your neighbours or look around where you live and I promise you there will be someone, somewhere that needs your help. Take the challenge and see the difference it will make in your life.

The consistent theme of modern research is that happiness; contentment, joy, love, appreciation and good moods have a positive effect on our mental and physical health! Conversely negative moods anxiety and consistent stress have a detrimental effect on our health.

Finally the link between happiness and health has been signed sealed and delivered!

- We can be directly responsible for 40% of our happiness.

- Happiness is a skill that can be learned!

- Happiness isn't found in more of... but in life's simple pleasures.

- Happy people live longer -it's good for your health.

- We need to change our outlook on life.

- Don't miss the miracles!

- Don't compare what you have with others.

- Appreciate what you have - count your blessings.

- Concentrate on what went right.

- Develop a strategy for coping with stress.

- Take control, de-clutter and organize better.

- Have lots of additives.

- Discover what you are good at and do more of it.

- Loving and Serving others brings you the most happiness.

- Get involved with your community, or like-minded people.

4

How it all worked out for me.

 And so I come to the part of our time together where I tell you my story; how I connected with my local community and discovered that all this research is actually true.

I was always very scientifically minded at school and at home. My father introduced me to the wonders of the natural world at an early age, taking me for long walks every week, pointing out birds, insects and trees. All this gave me an enquiring mind. I believed in the Theory of Evolution because that's what I was taught at school and I had no reason to dispute it. I remember being devastated when I found out that there was no Father Christmas - he was just a mythical figure – and I promptly dismissed the baby Jesus stories in much the same way.

I loved passing on what I had learned and I held a weekly nature club in my street for all the kids. It disappointed me that at aged 10, they didn't know that the green pigment in leaves is called chlorophyll! This fascination with biology carried on in high school where I became known as 'Su the science guru.' In particular, as we got into our teens, my girlfriends wanted my scientific knowledge on menstruation, how to relate to boys etc. One day, I noticed that my friend Carol had very sore, chapped lips, a condition that lasted for weeks. No one wanted to kiss her I can tell you that much! I was reading a popular teen magazine of the time called *Jackie* and the Cathy and Claire problem page seemed to have the answer to Carol's lingering lip problem. A small section right at the bottom was headed *labia*. I read with interest that this was a thickening of the lips, a common occurrence amongst teenage girls which would affect all of us. I thought it made sense because Carol's lips did look as if they were growing thicker. I immediately told all my chums that her labia plight would eventually befall us too but it was nothing to worry about. Three days later I was called to the Year 5 Head's office and she asked me why I was spreading such hurtful information around the school about Carol. I explained that I was reporting a scientific fact and wondered why it was such a big deal. She then explained that the term *labia* referred to the vaginal lips not the lips on our mouths. Wow, I got that wrong! It's true that a little knowledge is a dangerous thing.

I was always the last to do anything in my school year so I reached the age of 16 without ever having kissed a boy. My friend Michelle noticed that the Michael Jackson poster on my bedroom wall had a hole where his mouth should have been and this was because I would go up to it each evening and kiss him, gradually wearing the paper away. I'd done the same with my pillow having a threadbare place right where my head hit it as I kissed imaginary boys. When I confessed all this to my friend she gave me the most pitying look. A few days later she told me she'd spoken to a lad called David and arranged for him to give me a snog in an old bashed up VW Beetle that everyone used for courting! Perhaps she thought I was grateful but I was actually sick with dread but I knew I had to conquer my fear. I duly reported to the arranged place and David made it abundantly clear that he was just doing me a favour. Who said romance was dead?! I went cold when he put his arm around my shoulders and as his open mouth loomed towards me, I let out an almighty scream and bolted out of the car. Poor lad, I must have frightened him to death! I hope I didn't give him a complex all his life. Eventually, I had my first kiss at a party when I was a little tipsy but I've a horrible feeling it was with Michelle! Even though I got over my phobia of kissing I found I was never asked out on a date. All my boyfriends were just that – boys that were friends. At a disco, I remember a gorgeous blond guy asking me if I was getting up for a dance. Excitedly I said, 'Yes' and stood up only for him to shout over to his mates, 'C'mon lads we can sit 'ere.'

I had 2 serious boyfriends before meeting this lad called Tony. I can't say I fell in love with him but he seemed good fun and 3 years later we were married. Tony never proposed, we just got carried along with the excitement of doing something new in our lives. All the time though, I never felt as if I knew what love was. I remember telling my friend Karen that I had doubts about getting married and she said I should call it off. This was a week before getting hitched and as most of the wedding gifts had already arrived, I just couldn't face the upheaval and explanations. I put it down to wedding

190

nerves and thought everyone probably felt like that. So I went ahead.

We were both busy building our sales careers and some nights I didn't see Tony until after 9pm. I became very selfish, arranging things to suit myself. Tony was working in a demanding sales environment and the stress made him very volatile. We trundled on like this for 3 years and I just assumed that this was how marriage turned out for everyone. Family and friends were asking when we were going to start a family and around December 1983, I started feeling broody. I was very excited at the prospect and it gave me a fresh view of what our marriage could be like if we were parents.

It was the New Year and Tony was about to start a new well-paid job; if I wanted to give up work it would be a good time. He went on a month's training course in Birmingham, coming home each weekend. At the end of January he dropped a bombshell and told me he'd never really loved me and wanted a divorce. Apparently, he'd met some fun people at his new job and wanted to be single again. It was such a shock! I wasn't mentally prepared. If he'd said it in November I'd have told him I felt the same but, in my mind, I had just made a big commitment to him. I was being dumped by my husband who had never loved me so, as you can imagine, my self-esteem hit rock bottom.

It was too much to bear and I went home to my mum and dad's to be consoled. My mum had always said the marriage wouldn't last but I didn't listen and now she was being proved right. We always know best don't we? Nevertheless, my parents were amazing and welcomed me back with open arms. They decided they would move house to give us more space as my old room had become a sitting room. Tony said he would move to his parents' house when they went to Australia in a couple of months and in the meantime, we would just live separate lives in the house until it was sold.

I loved my job and I was good at it so I threw myself into work. I started to think positively about my life and made plans to become a writer. I had a little daydream that I would write a best-selling book and I used to imagine untold success to the tune of *Wishful Thinking* by China Crisis. I had it all acted out in my head like a pop video. It was a very frightening time for me but these positive thoughts kept me going. Many of my best friends were still about town and I began to return to my old life in readiness for the months ahead. By then, it was the end of February; a month had passed and Tony had been away most weekends having fun with his newfound work colleagues.

One evening he arrived home when I was in bed and came straight upstairs into the bedroom. When he asked me if I was awake, I just wanted to ignore him but there was something different about his tone of voice so I wondered what on earth he could possibly have to say to me. To my astonishment, he told me that he'd become a born-again Christian and wanted to start over again with our marriage. He'd given his life to God and God didn't want him to get divorced. WHAT!!!

Tony had always had a faith of sorts. I often heard him saying his prayers on the loo at night as he smoked his last cigarette before bed. He had been a choirboy at primary school but apart from that he'd never mentioned religion. He had met a Christian in his new job and unbeknown to me, had been doing a Bible study. He began to explain that everyone has a God-shaped hole in their heart and people try to fill it with all sorts of material things and experiences but a relationship with God is the only thing that will satisfy all our desires in life.

At this point, I thought he'd had a hole drilled in his head and some weird cult had filled it with mumbo-jumbo. It meant nothing to me – I was badly hurt and nothing was going to change that especially some religious nutcase who was moving out in 2 months. No way! I was just starting to get my life back together and feeling confident and positive about my future life as a single woman. I told Tony it was too late; our marriage couldn't be put right and it was over.

Over the next few weeks, he persisted by dropping in bits of information about this new-found purpose in his life and something began to rest in my soul. I don't really know why I stopped blaspheming but I realised that I didn't want to offend this God. He seemed so real to Tony. He brought the person of Jesus Christ to life. Tony explained that we are all sinners but I didn't know what that meant. He said that God created the world and although His creation was perfect, the devil tempted the first man Adam and sin was brought into the world. Everybody – him and me included – carries this original sin which taints us and separates us from God, just as Adam and Eve were separated from Him when they were cast out of the Garden of Eden. But God had provided a way to be forgiven so that we could have a relationship with Him if we accepted His plan of salvation for our lives and trust in the fact that His only son, Jesus Christ was born to be sacrificed on a cross to pay the price for our sins. A few memories came back about this from my Sunday school days but I hadn't paid much attention as I only went to chase a lad I fancied. Tony went on to explain that in the Old Testament, people would sacrifice an animal or a bird to atone for their sins. God told them it was a temporary measure until the day that He would do something to restore His relationship with them. Jesus' death was part of God's divine plan to save humanity and acquit us all forever. We can receive that forgiveness if we accept Jesus and believe that He died for our sins. When we die, we will join Him in Heaven where He lives with God. In the meantime the Holy Spirit would come and live in me, helping me everyday.

Phew, that was a lot to take in! I found it hard to believe because I was taught that the world came together in a big bang. I asked questions about this and Tony would go away and always find the answer. So I asked more and more questions as the weeks went on.

Something was happening right before my eyes that I couldn't ignore. Tony was becoming the sweetest person to live with - happy, joyful, relaxed, loving gestures and kind words. There was something in this Christian malarkey but I wasn't sure whether it was for real.

At the end of April, he asked if I would go to church. Tony had been slipping off to church every Sunday morning about 9am and not getting back until 12.30pm full of the joys of spring! What the heck was he doing? When I used to go as a child it was all over in 70 minutes. We used to stay in bed until 1pm but now, he was up bright and early, so I thought I'd give it a try. There was nothing else to do in those days - no Sunday shopping or TV!

I remember walking into this old shoe factory that had been converted into a church. Everybody seemed to know my name and was really friendly. I had 3 questions in my head and incredibly, the preacher answered them all and seemed to look straight at me as he answered them as if he knew what was in my mind. I was bowled over by the friendship these people showed me because it was such a stark contrast to my dog-eat-dog working environment in sales where people would do anything to be successful. Backstabbing and bad-mouthing colleagues was the norm.

I began going to church each week learning more about this incredible God that had done all this for me and wondering why no one told me until I was 24 years of age. I got all my scientific questions answered and Tony asked me why I wouldn't take the last step of faith and ask for God's forgiveness. I felt rather pressured but I couldn't think of a reason *not* to and by July, still feeling unsure, I said a prayer in the shower one morning as I got ready for work. When I told Tony he started phoning people to tell them as if I had just given birth!

That summer was the best in my life. I finished working as I had burned out with all the stress and began to learn more about God's love. The church became my extended family and we worked together on community projects. I felt engaged with life and totally fulfilled with a newfound purpose that delivered genuine friendships.

By September, I was wondering whether the prayer I had said in July had done anything spiritually. I remember reading in Corinthians, a book in the New Testament, that if the Spirit of God was living in you then you would be able to understand the Bible. Well I could and it dawned on me that everything I read made a great deal of sense and I danced around our living room with joy!

Tony and I fell in love with each other as God worked on our selfish ways and we became new people. At long last, I knew what it was to be in love and feel loved and cherished in return. All that was 32 years ago and I've not regretted a thing.

I hope that the things I've shared resonate with you. A painful journey but one that reaches a great destination - Heaven. If you would like to say the prayer of forgiveness, I've provided it below for you to say in your own time.

We have been working on confident thinking in this little book and I can also tell you that my confidence has grown from knowing God.

Dear God,

I'm sorry for all of my sins. I put my trust in Jesus Christ alone as my Lord and Saviour. Please forgive me, and help me turn from everything I know to be wrong. Now I ask your Holy Spirit to come into my heart and mind. I receive your gift of everlasting life.

In Jesus' name I pray.

Amen.

When you've said this prayer, get a Bible and start reading it <u>every day</u> and God will speak to you through it supernaturally. Find a local church where you can become part of the family of God and flourish.

Every blessing.

Su Ainsworth

If you would like to email me about anything you've read, you are welcome to contact me at <u>confidencegym@gmail.com</u>

A book like this would not have been completed without the help of several individuals in my life.

Thank you to:

- **Carol Halton** who started Confidence Gym with me back in 2006.
- My girls' **Church Life Group** who unknowingly, were my guinea pigs as I tested out all my material.
- To **my best friends.** You know who you are so thank you for spurring me on with regular encouragement.
- To my fantastic editor, **Jackie Dickinson**, without whom you would be reading a poorer version of this book.
- **Graham Clarke** for all things publishing wise.
- My **small writers' group** for their helpful advice.
- The **3 people** who have taken time to read through and endorse this book. (See back cover)
- To **everyone I've ever had a spot of bother with**. I would never have learned as much without the odd crisis!
- Special thanks to my **dear husband Tony,** who constantly allows me to be me, and my wonderful **son James**, my greatest work so far.
- I'd be nothing without the input of a wise **mum and dad** who gave me a brilliant childhood on which to build my confidence.
- Finally, thanks to the **Lord God** for His continuous love and guidance every day. You have made known to me the path of life.

Sound Bite Testimonials.

Don't just take my word for it, look what others have said about Confidence Gym.

"I WOULD 100% RECOMMEND IT. I THINK THE ADVICE IS ESSENTIAL FOR ALL AREAS OF LIFE!" **Laura.**

"AN ENJOYABLE EXPERIENCEAND LEARNING AT THE SAME TIME" **Marie.**

"MY CONFIDENCE HAS GROWN AND MY HEALTH IS IMPROVING SLOWLY BECAUSE OF THE POSITIVE THINKING" **Gill.**

"CHALLENGING", **Shiranee.**

"IT'S BRILLIANT, CHALLENGING AND REACHABLE" **Andrea.**

" YES THIS HAS DIRECTLY BENEFITTED MY DAY TO DAY LIFE-ITS BEEN GREAT AND I'M SAD ITS FINISHED" **Andrea.**

"HAS HELPED WITH EVERY DAY SITUATIONS- I COULD GO ON!!

"SHOWED ME A REFRESHING OUTLOOK ON LIFE" **Carolyn.**

"GO WITHOUT HESITATION" **Gina.**

"BRILLIANT, GREAT FUN, LOTS OF LAUGHS AND LIFE CHANGING TIPS" **Celanie.**

"IT'S VERY EYE OPENING AND REALLY WORKS" **Michaela.**

"I'VE FELT BETTER ABOUT MYSELF THAN I HAVE FOR A LONG TIME" **Linda.**

"IT'S FOR ANY WOMAN AT ANY STAGE OF LIFE" **Diane.**

"LOTS OF GREAT ADVICE AND A VAST AMOUNT OF WISDOM" **Kath.**

"REALLY TAYLORED TO A WOMANS NEEDS AND INTERESTS" **Rachael.**

"IT DOES WHAT THE TITLE SUGGESTS, ENHANCING YOUR LIFE IN MANY WAYS AND INCREASES YOUR SELF ESTEEM" **Corrina.**

"A MUST COURSE FOR EVERYONE" **Vicky.**

"IT COVERED SUBJECTS THAT HAVE BEEN OF RELEVANCE AT THIS STAGE OF MY LIFE" **Linda.**

"YOU'D LOVE IT!" **Valerie**

See what others have to say!

'Inspirational', 'Compelling' and 'Exuberant' are but a few words I could use to describe this masterclass in the art of self - confidence. Su's natural and spirited delivery of this course packs a real punch when it comes to the careful unpicking of the insecurities that hang like an anchor in many of our lives. Confidence Gym is the ideal companion to kick start the journey to self - discovery and a stronger more confident you, powerfully reminding us that we all deserve to feel good about ourselves.
Michelle Walker, LSAlevel 3 Teacher. Standish High School.

As modern women, regardless of our background, ability or beliefs we all want to feel fulfilled, happy, confident and valued, no matter how we choose to spend our time and energy; whether in a professional capacity or being an amazing momma and wife. In her own unique and engaging style and drawing on personal experience and a natural 'God given talent, Su has been passionately speaking 'life' into 1000's of women's' lives for the past 10 years. Her discerning observations, little nuggets of insight and 'joie de vivre' (not forgetting her practical toolkit) will encourage you to step-out boldly and begin embracing life head-on, transforming yourself into the beautiful and captivating women you were always intended to be! Sit back and enjoy the ride.
Cath Stanley, Business and Marketing Consultant.

I took part in Confidence Gym during a time I doubted myself a lot. After leaving Uni I was unable to find work and was stuck in a dead end job unable to leave my parents house. However after attending Confidence Gym the session made me realize how grateful I am to have supportive parents and a roof over my head, even if it wasn't my own. I'm young and have my whole life ahead of me, just one session helped me to realize this and has kept me going through this difficult time.
Hannah Winstanley. University graduate of Television & Radio production.

From giving me the confidence to communicate to loads of toddlers and their mums with a glove puppet bunny to informing me of the research into the importance of the first five years of my children's lives in setting their confidence level; Confidence gym has proved invaluable to me in dealing with the challenges and transitions in life.
Rachel Alcock, Mum & Part time events assistant.

I have known Su Ainsworth for over 12 years and have had the privilege of taking part in 'Confidence Gym' twice - once with my Daughter and once with a friend. The experience in each case was wonderful. Sessions were full of fun, laughter and well presented ideas, based on sound scientific and biblical principles and delivered in Su's friendly, welcoming and encouraging style. Her love for people, her passion to empower women with the tools necessary to succeed in life and the assurance that our true worth and value is found in our Heavenly Father never fail to change lives for the better. Go girl! You & 'Confidence Gym' are awesome!
Di Taylor (Company Partner, Master Lock & Safe)

Dear Su, Just a line to say thank you for all the confidence Gyms. They were really fantastic and I just had a brilliant time and a good laugh! Also it has made me see many things in daily life in a new light and a fresh attitude! Thank you for all the weeks of preparation you obviously put into it, and your presentations were superb! Feeling flattered now? - So you should because you were great. Love **Jill Jopson.**

I was both nervous and intrigued on arriving at "the Confidence Gym", and a room full of ladies I didn't know. Within the next few hours, the clever and interactive organization brought everyone happily together. There was no judgment, no pride or embarrassment. The exercises were fun, the time flew by. The positivity that radiated around the room was phenomenal. All were blessed with laughter and wellbeing.
In a world of insecurity and judgement, where women struggle to gain and keep their personal value. Susan Ainsworth's confidence gym, is a breath of fresh air, both creative and uplifting: reminding us all that we are strong, special and loved, and we don't need to be validated by peers or society to believe this. Thank you Susan, long may it continue.
Mandy Lee, Design Director. Marshalls Preston.

I was fortunate to attend a Confidence Gym run by Su Ainsworth in 2012. What a blessing it was! During a gentle afternoon with lots of laughter and a good measure of God's Word, Su inspired us to be more positive and to 'go for it'; she encouraged us to walk with God and live life to the full. At the start of our afternoon, Su told us that that she felt that the Lord had gifted her in the area of building confidence. I would wholeheartedly agree! Grounded firmly and deeply in her Christian faith and her love for God, Su delivers with great warmth and wit, thoughtfulness and encouragement, enthusiasm and assurance. Su welcomes participants warmly; gently takes them out of their comfort zone; encourages learning through a variety of fun and enjoyable activities; shares helpful strategies and tips for building self esteem and confidence; provides food for further personal reflection and signposts a variety of useful reading and resources. I followed up the reading and radio resources and these have not only helped to build my confidence, but have also enriched my own faith in God and, indeed, they continue to do so.

All in all, Su's Confidence Gym was an interesting and enjoyable afternoon with very worthwhile learning. Affirming, empowering and, for me, life-changing. I would recommend Su's Confidence Gym without hesitation to anyone who is seeking help with building his or her confidence and self-esteem.
Christine Durber Retired.

Su, I would just like to take this opportunity to thank you for your inspiration and enthusiasm. It is great to learn that everyone else thinks the same. You've really made my life a lot more how I wanted it to be. To great times to come. **Gemma.**

This has been so spot on for me to come on. God has been teaching me to start making goals again and to be a confident person now I feel I have the tools to really get stuck in. You are such a fun, enthusiastic – lovely person and I'm sad this has finished. Thank you. **Andrea.**

I would recommend Confidence gym to everyone, even if you feel confident already. I guarantee you will feel even more so by going along. You will have great fun as well as learning Su's tips, tricks and advice, which you can then put into practice in your own life.
Jenny Berrill, Researcher.

I enjoyed Confidence Gym. As an instructor your delivery is smooth, confident and professional. Your sense of the positive is a joy to experience. You seem to be a product of your scientific research and it's application combined with your experience of life. The Confidence Gym always delivers a positive message grounded in biblical truths. It has been described as 'enjoyable', 'inspiring' and 'uplifting' by past attendees. Thank you Su and long may its message continue.
Janet Blackledge, Church warden, All Saints' Church, Higher Walton, Preston.

Self-Confidence is something we can all lack in our lives, it's very easy in today's society to find ourselves in a negative spiral. Su talked about how we can change our own habits and are in control of our own destiny. You will walk away from Su's course feeling inspired,

invigorated and wanting to make positive life choices.
Natalie Lawrence. HLSA Teacher. Standish High School.

This course helped me to think of the important things in life. Su spoke about how low self-esteem effects people in different ways, this helped me realise that the habits that I have now and the decisions I make because of those habits shape the person I will be 5 years from now. Su inspired me to think positive about the small things and this has helped improve my wellbeing and my confidence has flourished
Claire Hatton. HSLA Teacher. Standish High school.

Su ran several Confidence Gym sessions for a girls lunchtime club I run in a secondary school. The teaching was very insightful and practical. The content was applicable to young girls, as well as adults, and empowered and equipped them to feel more confident in themselves and their abilities. The illustrations and activities made the messages memorable, especially as confidence is something teenage girls struggle with. A lot of the girls took on Su's advice, feeding back what they had done differently in the week - they still talk about the sessions a year later. I have seen them become able to engage in conversation more confidently and walk with their head held high!
Rebecca Robinson. Youth Worker, Longton Community Church, Preston.

Bookings.

Confidence Gym can be adapted to a single session or a whole weekend event! If you would like to book me to speak at one of your events please email confidencegym@gmail.com

Confidence Gym Bibliography

This list is by no means complete. I borrowed many books from the library for which there is no record. I've watched countless TV shows, documentaries and read newspaper and Web reports whilst researching my topics. Some of the books listed haven't contributed anything to this book but were ones that I think you might like.

THE HOLY BIBLE
CONFIDENCE BOOSTERS
Martin Perry ISBN 0-600-61323-2 Hamlyn (Octopus Publishing)
BATTLE FOR THE MIND
Stephen Matthew ISBN 0-9538516-3-X Interprint Creative Solutions
NOT ANOTHER SELF-HELP BOOK
Dr David Fong   ISBN 1-84205-489-9 Geddes and Grosset
SUCCESS INTELLIGENCE
Robert Holden ISBN 0-340-83017-4 Hodder & Stoughton
CHANGE YOUR THINKING
Dr Sarah Edelman ISBN 0091906954 Vermilion Press
DEADLY EMOTIONS
Dr Don Colbert ISBN 978-0785267430 Thomas Nelson Inc
THE PURPOSE DRIVEN LIFE
Rick Warren ISBN 978-0310335511 Inspirio Zondervan
THE POWER OF HABIT
Charles Duhigg ISBN 978-1-847-94624-9
HOW TO BE HAPPY
Liz Hoggard ISBN 0563493208 BBC Books
QUIRKLOLOGY
Prof Richard Wiseman ISBN 978-0-230-70215-8 Pan Macmillan
59 SECONDS
Prof Richard Wiseman ISBN 978-0-330-51160-5 Pan Macmillan
THE POWER OF YOUR SUBCONCIOUS MIND
Dr Joseph Murphy ISBN 978-1-4165-1156-4 Wilder Publications
INSTANT CONFIDENCE
Paul McKenna ISBN 0-593-05535-7 Bantam Press
HOW TO BE THE PERFECT HOUSEWIFE
 Anthea Turner ISBN 978-0-7535-1285-2 Virgin Books
PERSUASION
James Borg ISBN 978-0-273-71299-2 Pearson Books
PREDICTABLY IRRATIONAL
Dan Ariely ISBN 978-0-00-725653-2 Harper Collins
BLINK
Malcolm Gladwell ISBN 978-0-14-101459-3 Penguin
POSITIVITY
Barbara Fredrickson ISBN 978-1-85168-7-790-9 One World Publications
THE POWER OF FOCUS
J Canfield, M V Hansen and L Hewitt ISBN 978-0-091-87650-0 Vermilion Press
THE PSYCHOLOGY OF ACHIEVEMENT
Brian Tracy ISBN 978-1905453023 Nightingale Conant/Simon & Schuster
(available as audio book and audio CD)
Audio CD of Seminar called *WHO SWITCHED OFF MY BRAIN* by Dr Caroline Leaf.
Books by J.John & Mark Stibbe. A Box of Delights. A Bucket of surprises, A Barrel of fun, & A bundle of Laughs.

Also available by Su Ainsworth.

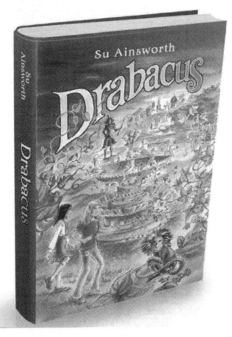

Holiday pals Susan Dean, Pauline and Michael are propelled into an adventure only possible in their wildest dreams when an old service elevator is discovered in the disused part of the Hotel.

The secret lift operator involves them in a 64-year-old mystery where only their intelligence and wisdom reveals a more sinister side to the whole affair. Who is the bizarre character they encounter and why does his power reach across time and affect us here and now? Will these four young minds be able to reveal his cunning strategy and save Drabacus?

Read on before it's too late, because our world may be in danger next.

Drabacus review on Amazon. Stacilou 17 June. 2014.

What a fantastic book I couldn't put it down! it's gripped me all the way through. Curious at first as the characters developed and then once they were in trouble because well I didn't stop reading till it was finished. The light hearted humour throughout the book was mingled with the excitement and tension of the adventure as the mystery unfolded. A great book for young and old at heart and it's left wide open for another adventure hope so!

Why I wrote this book.

I was listening to a sermon in church one day and was struck by the words:

Because the poison of the ordinary has deadened your senses to the magic of the moment.

I suddenly realised that this was true for me and wondered how this had come to be.

I set about thinking and was amazed to realise that this had happened very slowly over time. This book explains how it occurs and how to combat this erosion of your free will in the context of a story that is applicable to children and adults alike.

I wrote it whilst pregnant with my son and then left it on the shelf for 16 years so I know what it's like to become a victim of the **agent of familiarity**. If you give it some thought I think you may have too.

My aim is to make you aware that this force is at work and give you the tools to fight him.

For children aged between 8 and 12.

Order it from Amazon direct in paperback or kindle edition.

Also available from some good bookshops.

Enquiries to the author:
erasmusdrab@gmail.com

Printed in Great
Britain
by Amazon